LOOKING AHEAD

LOOKING AHEAD

The Realities of Aging:
Face Them with Faith

Enjoy!

Margaret J. Anderson

Margaret J. Anderson

CONCORDIA

Publishing House
St. Louis

The author expresses her thanks to Dr. V. S. Todd, Turlock, Calif., for reviewing the medical information in this manuscript. She expresses gratefulness, too, to Mr. Gilbert Moody, attorney, Turlock, Calif., and to Mr. Howard Kanter, financial adviser, Novata, Calif., for checking the legal and financial information in Chapter 3.

Contents

Preface

My husband and I were driving to Minnesota, where I was to speak at a Minneapolis writers' conference. We had spent the previous weekend with relatives in Kansas. We spoke of our delightful visit, expressed concern for an aunt who, because of Parkinson's disease, had aged considerably since we last saw her.

Musing I said, "I wonder what we will be like when we grow old."

My husband, who is older than I, chuckled. "Old?" he countered. "We are old, at least I am."

I denied the fact. Healthy and active, to me he looked 10 years younger than many men his age. Nevertheless we began to speak about age, about our future, and about how we would cope should one of us become ill and die.

We had driven some distance into Iowa when I sensed my husband's speech had changed. Slurred, his words sounded as if they came from a man who was intoxicated.

"Something's radically wrong," he said. "The left side of my face feels numb." He pulled to the side of the road and handed me the car keys. "Here, you drive."

Frightened, I took the wheel. I suspected a stroke. What will I do? I thought. How will I cope?

I suggested we head for the nearest motel, contact a doctor, then work out plans from there.

Fortunately the stroke proved to be a mild one, affecting only the left side of my husband's face. As we worked out problems connected with the incident, I was reminded of this book assignment for which I had already done considerable research.

I realized the mild stroke was a symptom of growing old, and I didn't like it. I preferred to detain old age. The English author Jonathan Swift understood such reluctance. He said: "Everyone desires to live long, but no one wants to grow old."

In attendance with a group of women concerned about the elderly poor, I once viewed a filmstrip which portrayed the story of an elderly woman who tenderly cared for some beans she had planted in a flower pot and placed on the window ledge of her one-room apartment.

When the pods appeared, she realized the pot was too small. Stealthily she took the plant to a nearby parkway, where she planted it among the border flowers. The tender care continued.

Then disaster struck. Before she could harvest her crop, city workmen mowed the area—flowers, grass, and bean plant.

Digging frantically among the debris, the woman managed to retrieve a few pods. The closing scene showed her splitting the pods, gathering the beans, and pushing them gently into a pot of new soil.

Every time I recall this scene I feel shame, shame that so many of us older persons, though we can anticipate so much more than a few beans in a pot, fail to face the future with this type of hope.

In the coming years, gerontologists claim, we can expect to live longer and better than we have before.

Cancer researchers are excited about the possibility of a breakthrough in their field. Other researchers are learning about cures for strokes, heart attacks, blindness, and deterioration of the nervous system.

Some are concerned about the quality of life—education, retraining, and meaningful employment. One writer speaks of the concept of "retirement villages" being replaced by "second-career villages."

At 71 Dr. Karl Menninger said: "The opportunities in life have not diminished—they have multiplied. To me the end of life is not stretching out on a chaise lounge. . . . I want to be going, contacting people, moving."

Though he acknowledged the dangers in the world that he didn't like, he still believed life is essentially good.

Harold Dye speaks of the ability of the elderly to change what isn't right: "We so-called senior citizens in this country have enough political clout to do anything we choose to do. We can turn our world right side up."

The late Dr. Edward Stieglitz wrote: "The longer men live,the more time there is to think; to think is to grow; and to grow is to live." In this context we can adopt the philosophy of the Greek Diogenes, who lived to be 89. When friends tried to persuade him to curtail his activities and slow down, he said, "What? If I were running in a stadium, should I slow my pace when I approach the goal?"

Let's go back to the bean story for a moment. Note, the woman's faith in a future bean harvest can be said to have dual implications. Her actions evidence a faith and a trust in God who, after the Flood, told Noah: "While the earth remaineth, seedtime and harvest, and cold and heat, and summer and winter, and day and night shall not cease" (Genesis 8:22). When God created the world, He established a dependable order.

One theologian says God's faithfulness "spans the world like a rainbow. We don't have to build it, we only need to live under it."

Knowing God is always there helps us face stress, money problems, illness, yes even death, with fortitude and hope.

A Japanese author said that if only we knew when old age was coming to call we would bolt the door and say, "Not at home."

This is impossible. Unless we die, we do grow old. And because we do, we need to know how to cope with problems of health, one of which is a stroke; loss of spouse; a reduced

9

income; loneliness—whatever we may face. That's what this book is all about.

For the most part I will be addressing *you*, the reader. Yet I intend the word to be inclusive, to refer also to loved ones for whom you will need to cope as they grow old.

Margaret J. Anderson

LOOKING AHEAD

1

Who Is Old?

Shortly after I graduated from high school an aunt who had just celebrated her 50th birthday died as a result of cerebral hemmorhage.

"How tragic," relatives and friends lamented. "And to think she was so young!"

Young? I didn't agree. I thought of her as a relatively old woman. But I changed my mind when I reached my 50th birthday. Wasn't I the same person I had always been? True, my life-style had changed to a certain extent. My children had established homes of their own. My husband and I missed them. But I was as busy as I had ever been. No, I thought, I am not old.

Who then is old?

It all depends. Gerontologists tell us age is relative. We cannot box a particular segment of society into a neat package and say, "These people are old." Such labels stereotype; they do not perceive.

Most of us feel that we are the same people we have always been, even though our life-styles may have changed or we may suffer from some disease or infirmity. A person 60, 70, or 80 years old carries within him feelings, knowledge, desires, temperament with which he was identified before he reached this age.

Again, who is old?

Aristotle claimed the body is in its prime from 30 to 35 years of age, the mind at 49. Today life expectancy is much higher than it was in Aristotle's day. Yet this man understood that mind and body do not always age at the same rate. Regardless of chronological age, a person may

13

appear very old physically yet be relatively young psychologically. This is particularly true when disease or infirmity strike. During her 30s and 40s Janet Brown aged considerably physically because of multiple sclerosis. Yet she remained as young mentally as she had ever been. The same could be said of persons who suffer from severe arthritis or other subversive diseases.

Psychological Aging

Someone has said we are old *psychologically* when we quit learning. We are young in proportion to our quest for knowledge. Our local librarian attests to this fact when she lists the many books one resident, an 85-year-old retired teacher, checks out each week.

When Charles Kettering, automotive genius, was asked why, at age 70, he was embarking on a whole new inquiry into scientific problems, he answered, "Why shouldn't I be interested in the future? I'm going to live in it!"

We are old psychologically, too, when we become inflexible to change. Recently I heard a Sunday school leader lament the fact that some of his teachers were so reluctant to adopt and make use of modern teaching aids: films, slides, overhead projectors, resource books, and periodicals. "Strange thing," he said, "I have a teacher of an adult class who is close to 80. He routinely sparks his teaching by using one or more of these tools. It's no wonder his class is the most popular and well attended in our adult department."

A tolerant attitude toward new experiences, flexibility toward change, curiosity about the unknown, a realistic acceptance of misfortune—these are the characteristics which identify delayed psychological aging. It has been said: "Some people die at 30 and are buried at 70."

So you see the psychological age, except in instances of mental dysfunction, may be measured in terms of how a person experiences life. The psychologically old set up dead-end blocks to creative living; the psychologically young tear them down.

14

Sociological Aging

Whichever, sociologists working in the field of gerontology tell us *our attitudes* as we age are determined to a large extent by experiences we have had. My husband and I consider ourselves thrifty, work-disciplined individuals. We think thrice before we patronize an expensive restaurant. We shop discriminately. Why? I was in my late teens and early 20s, my husband serving his first church, when our country suffered one of its worst depressions. Shortly before we were married Franklin Delano Roosevelt declared a "bank holiday." As a result we kissed our meager savings good-bye. We made do or did without—on a salary equivalent to what today's youth might spend on a night out.

Were you to poll members of our peer group, you would find many people very much like us. Representing the same generation cohort, they react to life in the same way we do because they have lived through tight-money experiences.

Physical Aging

Physical aging is determined largely by the extent disease, dissipation, or infirmity have taken their toll.

At 35 a brilliant woman, a former drug addict now rehabilitated and active in the church, looks and acts 20 years older than she is. In contrast I recall a healthy, energetic woman who kept house for her husband and son and sang in the church choir when she was 90. She looked close to 60.

Who is old?

If 65 is considered the cutoff point, a large number of people are old. A greater percentage who have reached this chronological age are living today than at any other time in history. A late U. S. census indicates that approximately one of 10 persons (over 21 million) is 65 years of age or over. This is 6½ times more than in 1900. By the year 2000 the anticipated figure, experts say, will be 28 million.

A child born at the turn of the century could be expected

to live to be 48 years old. A person born today can expect to reach 80. This means that persons who are 65 today can expect to live an additional 15 years, with women living several years longer than men.

Why do women live longer than men? Explanations differ. The most often suggested are:

1. A woman is born a more efficient machine, better able to cope with illness.

According to geneticists the xy combination of chromosomes, which determines maleness, possesses fewer safety factors than the xx combination of the female.[1] Because the male y chromosome has virtually no genes, it fails to balance any toxic genes that may accompany the x chromosome. Consequently the male fetus has a 120 percent greater chance of being spontaneously aborted. And, in the first weeks of life, 34 percent more boy than girl infants die. Further, more male than female children succumb to infectious diseases.

2. A woman less frequently suffers from heart malfunctions and ulcers.

For the most part these diseases are caused by stress. All through life the male competes. He ambitiously strives to achieve, to provide a good living for his family, to acquire status and prestige. Under such stress he is a more likely candidate for heart disease and ulcers. Usually he drinks and smokes more than women. He more frequently dies from cancer of the lungs as well as other cancers. In the future we can expect this trend to change, however, since women are becoming more competitive in the labor world and because they smoke and imbibe more than they used to.

3. Retirement may not be as shocking to women as to men.

Retirement doesn't end a woman's work. Normally she continues her homemaker role. Thus she is more relaxed at home. She is more apt, too, to have cultivated interests and hobbies that occupy her time.

4. "More women than men go to church, thus deriving peace and comfort."

This statement from a *Reader's Digest* author stresses the importance of faith in an older person's life. It's obvious that women's growing interest in the Bible (authenticated by the ever-increasing number of women's study groups), coupled with their consistent church atttendance, gives them an edge over men in coping with stress.

5. Women's work is usually less hazardous than men's.

Other Factors in Aging

Other factors also play a part in the aging process, whether a person be male or female. Take the concept of aging as a period of indolence, for instance. Being persuaded to look forward to empty years tends to cause a person to think of *old* and *useless* as synonymous terms. One who is expected to be unproductive may well assume such a role.

Yet there is no need to equate these terms. By refusing to do so, my husband served eight interim pastorates after he retired.

Aging is evidenced, too, when older persons are isolated from family or friends and when they begin to dwell in the past instead of anticipating the future. Closely associated with this aspect of aging is memory loss. Yet only a very small percent of older persons are forgetful or confused to the extent that they can be called senile.

Heredity also has an effect on length of life. You are apt to live as long as your forefathers. Both the parents and grandparents of the 90-year-old woman mentioned previously lived to be close to 100.

Dr. Alexander Leaf tells of visiting areas in the Caucasus, Kashmir, and Ecuador where people were reported to live exceptionally long lives.[2] Besides finding that heredity played an important role in the aging of these people, Dr. Leaf surmises their diet and their usually active lives contribute a great deal to their longevity.

Some gerontologists claim that married persons live longer than those who remain single.

Of course some facets of aging, accidents, and in some instances health, are beyond our control. Nevertheless, if we live long enough we will grow old.

Common Misconceptions

A study of aging would not be complete without a clarification of prevalent generalizations and misconceptions regarding older persons:

1. Most older persons are disabled.

Not so. Eighty-nine percent of all men and women over 65 live in the community and are totally self-sufficient. Many continue working beyond retirement age.

2. Most elderly persons suffer from mental deterioration.

Intelligence tests reveal little or no decline in knowledge and comprehension in the average older person. All things being equal, if we have good health we continue to store information as we age. Researchers believe the ability to think and reason may even increase with age. Our vocabulary may have doubled in the interim since we left high school or college. Old dogs do learn new tricks.

The difference between the use of the mind by the young and the old lies in the speed of response to stimuli. A younger person responds more quickly than does an older person, because it takes less time for him to retrieve information that he has stored in his mind. Given additional time, an older person reacts as competently, in some cases more so, than a younger person.

3. Most men and women over 65 are no longer interested or engage in sexual activity.

According to gerontologist Edward W. Busse, approximately 60 percent of older couples remain sexually active to age 75. Some sex researchers put the figure at 80 percent.

Sex may not play a preponderant role in an elderly

person's life, yet it is an urge that does not dissipate. Every human needs to be loved, touched, and esteemed regardless of age. The ability to respond sexually may diminish as men and women age. There are physical and psychological reasons why this is true.[3] Yet with tender, loving stimulation the ability to respond may remain indefinitely, a characteristic which is singularly typical of humans. Might not this indicate that God intended men and women to enjoy sex as well as to use it as a vehicle to reproduce themselves?

4. Retirement is an endless round of recreation, travel, and fun.

We need not scoff at recreation, travel, and fun. They are well-deserved prizes justly earned. Yet for the most part the elderly seek a balance between them and useful pursuits. Sweden's King Gustav V avidly pursued tennis at 69. Senator Theodore Francis Greene of Rhode Island used the Senate gymnasium more than most of his colleagues. An ardent boxer, he is said to have given up the sport at 86. Yet these two persons combined recreation and fun with useful pursuits.

5. Older people are all alike.

They are no more alike than all babies and all teenagers are all alike. Obviously some problems are common to all, as indicated in the section about generation cohorts, but many are uniquely individual. A gerontologist friend, Dr. Vern L. Bengtson, says: "There is so much variableness, so many different factors in aging, that the problems faced by one family may be quite different from those encountered in another."

Thus we note the elderly cannot be categorized. Their ages vary psychologically, sociologically, and physically. They refute many of the steriotyped opinions about them. Recognizing these facts will enable us to understand our individual problems and those of our loved ones so that, as we age, we will be better able to cope with them.

2

Where Should You Live?

No matter what our psychological, sociological, or physical age, when we retire, we and our loved ones must consider where and in what type of accommodations we should live. The following case histories pinpoint the differences in our needs.

John and Rebecca Painter have lived in the same house in southern Oregon since their wedding day. Now they realize it is too large for their needs. The huge lawn and garden demand attention John is unable to give them. They have contemplated selling their home and moving to the California Bay Area so they can be near their two married children. "We could purchase a mobile home or rent an apartment," they say. "But is such a move advisable?"

*   *   *

Pearle Yeager, a widow, owns a small home in Montana. Its resale value is negligible. Their children's college expenses cut a big swatch out of the Yaegers' savings. Mr. Yaeger's terminal illness gobbled up much of what was left. Disabling arthritis prompts Pearle to consider moving to a warmer climate. She wonders, however, where she can find housing she can afford.

*   *   *

Tom Bellows worked several years following his 65th birthday. Now he wants to take life easy. Polly, his wife, would like freedom from housework to pursure her hobby, oil painting. Tom and Polly contemplate moving into a lifetime-care retirement facility. They need assistance in making their choice.

* * *

Alexander Heinrich is a business executive whose work has required that he and his wife, Samantha, move frequently. They have the means and the inclination to enter a retirement facility. "But I don't want my life regimented," Alexander says. "I love to play golf, and my wife is a camera enthusiast."

* * *

Four situations, all relating to older persons' retirement-living concerns, any one of which you or a loved one may someday have to cope with. There are no pat answers to attendant problems. Solutions must be evaluated individually, with careful attention given to each person's financial resources, ability to adapt to change, options regarding types of facilities and their locations, basic goals, and personal preferences.

Elmer Otte advises individuals who face retirement to play-act retirement options and rehearse them well before final performance.[1] This is wise counsel, counsel you can appropriate in chosing a retirement-living facility.

Can You Adapt to Change?

As a start pretend you are John and Rebecca Painter. In this role it is important to find out how well you adapt to change. Would being near your children offset separation from long-time friends, relatives who may live near you, church and community ties that wear familiar and comfortable labels? It wouldn't for some people.

I recall two elderly sisters, one a retired nurse, the other a retired schoolteacher, who decided to move from their Michigan apartment to a Florida retirement complex. Knowing they belonged to a closely knit family, I asked, "Won't you be lost so far from your family and friends?" They didn't think so.

A short time after their move the nurse suffered an attack of shingles which was followed by a long period of depression. "I didn't realize I would be so lonely," she admitted.

Eventually the two women retraced their steps. When I last heard from them they were living in a retirement home in Michigan, where they enjoy the fellowship and loving concern so typical of their particular family.

You mentioned the possibility of selling your large house and purchasing a mobile home or renting an apartment. Will the sale of the house cover the cost of the type of mobile home you prefer in the Bay Area city where your children live? How do current expenses, taxes, insurance, and upkeep compare with apartment rents and mobile-home space assessments?

Your reluctance to make the move may indicate you prefer staying where you are. After all, Oregon is only a short plane flight from your children.

If you remain in Oregon you may consider purchasing a smaller house, one with a miniature lawn you could manage or hire someone to care for. Or you could rent an apartment in the area. Another option: convert a portion of your home into an apartment and rent the other portion.

Concern for Money and Health

Now step into the shoes which belong to Pearle Yaeger, who lives in a small home in Montana. As Pearle, you face two problems of great concern. Arthritis necessitates a move to a warmer climate. Whatever living arrangement you choose must of necessity be reasonably inexpensive. Because this is true, you may wish to consider a government-subsidized retirement facility.

For many years public housing served only low-income families with children. More recently this service has been extended to the elderly. In Massachusetts 100 of these units, most of them one-story houses attached to each other, provided safety equipment, laundry rooms, and recreational facilities. Residents must certify that family

22

income does not exceed a stipulated amount. Your ability to pay will determine the rent you are charged.

Available in small towns as well as in large cities, some are one-story structures as in Massachusetts. Others are high-rise structures which provide comfortable studio and one-bedroom apartments for persons on limited incomes.

In researching this type of housing I visited an 11-story government-subsidized high-rise in a neighboring city. I learned that rentals vary in different parts of the country. In this particular high-rise residents pay $132 for a one-bedroom apartment, $106 for a studio. Adjustments are made which lower or raise monthly rentals, depending on the amount of individual income.

The entire ground floor contains "community" facilities: offices, a dining room, a lounge, an assembly room, a library, a game room, and a room for arts and crafts. Meals, available five days a week, are contracted for on a monthly basis: $40 for dinner, $64 for dinner and brunch.

"I'm very happy here," one of the residents, a widow whose husband's long illness had gobbled much of their meager savings, told me.

"Is nursing care provided?" I asked.

"No. Residents must be able to take care of themselves. When I can't, I will move to a nursing home of some kind. In the meantime I'm going to enjoy the security, excellent companionship, and comfortable living I receive here at a price I can afford."

Having pretended you are Pearle Yaeger, you may decide this type of housing is for you.

Lifetime-Care Facilities

Next imagine you are Tom and Polly Bellows. You desire a more leisurely life, with the assurance you will receive lifetime care.

Lifetime care is a nonprofit retirement-living arrangement made available by philanthropic, fraternal, and religious organizations. Facilities range from luxurious high-rise apartments overlooking the Pacific Ocean to pleasant studio, one-bedroom, or two-bedroom apartments in dormitory-type structures. Lifetime care promises you a place to live, good meals, medical care, and recreational facilities as long as you live.

To enter such a facility you will be required to pay a *founder's* or *development* fee which, at the time of your death, will remain the property of the organization. Fees vary according to the accommodations chosen. You may pay from $10,000 to $16,000 for a studio, $12,000 to $24,000 for one-bedroom, $20,000, $30,000, or more for two-bedroom accommodations. Monthly charges vary from $250 to $400 per person. Usually the facility contains a central lounge for each apartment unit, a dining room, recreational and craft centers, a library, laundry equipment, and accommodations for the entertainment of private guests.

Examples are *The Good Shepherd Village,* Concordia, Mo.; *Covenant Village,* Turlock, Calif.; *Prairie Homestead Retirement Center,* Wichita, Kans.; and *Shell Point Village,* Fort Myers, Fla.

Make sure you check the stability of the sponsors of the facility in which you are interested, however. If it is privately owned, demand a financial statement from the developer and discuss it with your banker or lawyer. There have been instances where developers of such centers have absconded with entrance fees paid by the residents.

A Variety of Choices

Before making a final decision, however, pretend you are Alexander and Samantha Heinrich.

Having moved frequently, you are accustomed to change. Nevertheless one geographical area may appeal to you more than another because of its proximity to relatives and friends.

Let's assume, however, that distance from a familiar locale doesn't matter to you. Regardless, you will be forced to consider other concerns: climate preference, financial obligations, area cultural and recreational advantages, retirement-home services.

In many small cities along the east and west coasts, in large cities—wherever—comfortable privately owned residential hotels cater to retired persons. Operated as profit-making business ventures, they provide rooms or apartments with utilities, maid service, and recreational facilities included with the rental fee. Owners will arrange medical care if you want them to. In some instances meals are part of the package, in others they can be purchased in the hotel's cafeteria/dining room.

On the other hand, you may wish to investigate nonprofit apartment or small-cottage rental housing made available by church, philanthropic, and fraternal organizations for self-sufficient persons who cherish their independence. Utilities as well as recreation facilities are included in the rental charge. *Vine Court,* a center operated by four Congregational churches in Hartford, Conn., and the *Campbell-Stone Memorial Residence,* a six-story high-rise in Denver, Colo., are examples of this type of retirement option.

Though most organization-sponsored rental facilities maintain special arrangements with doctors and hospitals, you may be required to pay for such services unless they are included in the monthly rental fee.

Since you desire to live an unregimented life, one of the many retirement villages in our country may appeal to you. Though some retirement homes include the word *village* in their names, they don't represent the type of retirement option indicated here. A retirement village is a community of houses and apartments that resemble a small city, except that residents must be over 50 or 55 years of age. Villages do not require that a resident be retired, but because these facilities are usually located in California, Arizona, and Florida most residents have retired and left homes in other states so they can live leisurely in a warm climate.

Villages are customarily self-governing. *Sun City,* a

retirement village near Phoenix, Ariz., with its churches, banks, hospital, doctors' building, golf courses, and recreational buildings, has grown so rapidly it is now considered a large city.

Being Alexander and Samantha Heinrich, you may even consider retirement in a foreign country.[2] One of the chief advantages of such a choice is that the cost of living is usually lower than in the United States.

In recent years Mexico, Central America, some countries in South America, and Spain have become favorites for Americans with retirement incomes who wish to live abroad.

Before you make such a move, however, learn all you can about health care, medicine availability, stability of government, and cost of living. Be aware that transportation to and from your adopted country must be included in your retirement budget.

Like the Heinrichs my husband and I had never known an "abiding" home. Over the years we moved from one church manse to another. When my husband decided to terminate his last full-time pastorate to serve pastorless churches on a interim basis, we realized we had several decisions to make. Where would we live? In what kind of home? Where would we secure financing?

California's climate appealed to us as much as anything did. And because we appreciate family ties we decided to visit a city where my husband's sister's family and one of my cousins reside.

Upon arrival we looked at homes in the price range we felt we could afford. We investigated tax assessments, medical facilities, church and cultural advantages. When we felt completely satisfied the city would fulfill our needs, we purchased a home.

Three-Generation Family Living

This chapter would not be complete without reference to a retirement option which many persons find they may

26

wish to consider. It is described in the following case history.

Recently Carla Downing received a letter from her son James. "Mom," he wrote, "you know Ethel and I are concerned about your living alone. We have a plan we hope will please you. Will you come and live with us? We've decided to renovate our house to provide a studio apartment for you. It will be connected to and have access to our home, but there will also be a private exit.

"We want you to consider yourself a member of our family, maintaining the measure of privacy that best suits you. We may get in each other's hair occasionally, but we're assured that, with God's help, we can manage to live amiably together.

"Ethel says you can help her when you want to, but you never need to feel obligated to do so.

"Think it over—I've already drawn up renovation plans. I believe you will like what I have done."

Would Carla be taking advantage of her son's family if she moved in with them? Not according to Howard Whitman, well-know authority on human relations. He says: "Why shouldn't aging parents, if they have done their job raising their children and shouldered the burden of their education, be able to accept warmly and graciously a helping hand from those for whom they have toiled? Does the loyalty of children end after they have received all their parents can give—or is it not their turn to pay back?"[3]

When I asked Carla's daughter-in-law how she thought her three-generation family would cope, she answered optimistically: "We have a lot going for us. For one thing, we share a common faith. Accustomed to quiet, Jim's mother will soon learn our three active high-school/college youngsters don't walk around the house on tiptoe with their mouths closed. No matter, she can retire to her own quarters to listen to her radio or watch television at the sound level she prefers; read, write letters, or rest without being disturbed. I'm sure she won't always agree with the way we handle our lives, but she won't interfere. She's not that kind of person."

There I believe is the secret of a happy three-generation family: *She's not that kind of person.* How does Ethel know? Because her mother-in-law has never been that kind of person.

As we age we tend to become not less, but more like the persons we have always been. A selfish individual becomes increasingly demanding and egocentric. A lonely recluse grows more withdrawn. A friendly extrovert continues to make friends. Personalities make or break the harmony of a three-generation home.

Though I know several unhappy three-generation families, I know as many, if not more, which are successful.

Pretend you are Carla. What would you do? If you had a choice, would you move in with your son and his family? Or would you prefer to live with a surrogate family in a retirement facility where you could enjoy care, security, and companionship with your peers?

Carla chose to live with her son's family. She's that kind of person.

You may think of other options. Regardless, that which you choose should specifically suit your physical needs, your finances, and your personal preferences.

3

Pocketbook Worries

Many business firms and professional organizations attempt to prepare members for retirement by advising them to figure out retirement income, pensions, Social Security benefits, and investments so they can cope with economic problems as they grow old.

The problem: these people are still on a payroll. To them retirement appears light years away.

It isn't. Suddenly we are there. Of necessity we find we must take stock of our assets, income, and possible expenditures. Elmer Otte's, *Retirement Rehearsal Guidebook*[1] provides helpful advice as well as blank asset, income, and budget charts which we can use to assess our financial status.

In addition let's consider some of the pertinent questions retirees ask:

* Where can I get the best returns on my savings?
* Should I make a will?
* How do annuities differ from trusts?
* What are my employment options?
* How can I stretch my retirement dollars?
* How can I protect myself from frauds?

Earnings on Savings
Dividends from Stocks and Mutual Funds

No matter how large or small your retirement savings, you hope and pray their earnings will sufficiently supplement your Social Security and pension benefits.

A few years ago you were urged to buy common stocks and mutual funds to accomplish this feat. Inflation would,

29

experts claimed, push share prices and dividends up—enabling you to hold your own when the dollar's purchasing power fluctuated.

Such thinking has taken on a fairy-tale connotation in the last decade, however. Instead of rising prices and increased dividends, prices have often fallen, and in some instances dividends have faltered. The mutual fund investor appears to have suffered most. Nevertheless, new funds have developed that look promising.

If you are interested in making an investment at this time, you should look for a company that:

* Has a steady earnings growth.
* Represents a field attuned to the social and economic climate of our time.
* Is presently paying a reasonable dividend. A retired investor can't live on tomorrow's income.
* Has the stability and stature to weather economic storms.

Be careful, however. Before making investments of this kind, it would be a good idea to get advice from an honest professional in this field.

When a heart attack forced a business-executive friend to retire, he immediately set out to teach his wife how to protect and increase their stock investments. Soon widowed, this man's wife successfully weathered the recent market storm. She not only kept her investments intact, in many instances she increased them. Her book,[2] written after her husband died, provides personally tested investment advice which attests to the fact she learned her lessons well.

When I say some mutual funds appear attractive as high-income generators, I refer to an entirely new type of investment (or mutual) funds—money-market funds described by Barrons in terms of safety, liquidity, and yield.

Pioneered by *Reserve Fund* in 1971, these cash-asset funds operate like a bank, except that the investor buys their shares and obtains a much higher rate of interest than he can achieve on a passbook savings account.

These funds invest their money in relatively high-yielding bank Certificates of Deposit, and at times in banker's acceptances and short-term U. S. government securities. Being mutual funds, they appeal to persons who wouldn't have the large sum of money ordinarily needed to invest in high-interest government securities. In some instances only a $100 initial deposit and interval payments of as little as $25 may be made. Shares can be purchased directly from the fund and redeemed whenever needed with a few-day withdrawal notice.

Though interest rates may fluctuate, depending on current market trends, investors have realized as much as 8 and 10 percent. If an investor desires, he can ask that income be plowed back into the fund for reinvestment.

Interest

Just as dividends are paid to stockholders for the use of their money, interest is paid to lenders for the use of theirs.

Many retired persons depend on interest as their chief supplementary income even though rates may vary from year to year depending on the financial status of our country. It varies, too, according to the amount and duration of a specific deposit. In this kind of investment you may earn anywhere from 5 to 10 or more percent, depending on the current trend.

Savings and Loan Associations invite time-deposits of varying amounts, on which they pay interest rates according to the duration of the deposit. Money invested for 6 years may earn approximately 8 percent interest. Unless you have an adequate fund in a regular savings or checking account, however, you may not wish to commit yourself to a long-term savings investment. Though you may withdraw your deposit at any time, you will receive a lower rate of interest for an early withdrawal.

Corporation bonds with varying dates of maturity also provide interest income, though you run some risk here, too. Interest is forthcoming also from U. S. Treasury bonds, and from municipal bonds—the debt securities of states, counties, cities, school districts, and highways. Municipal bonds may entice because their interest is tax-exempt.

To successfully invest for interest income, look for the highest return with safety. Investments with the U. S. government, or guaranteed by it, are by far the safest. Those guaranteed by sound corporations and large banks rank a close second.

Wills

Should you make a will? Yes. You should consult your attorney and do it now while you are able. Don't assume that if you die intestate—without a will—your property will automatically go to your spouse. In many states as much as two thirds may be awarded to the children, or if there are no children, to your relatives.

A member of one of our parishes died intestate. The state stepped in and divided the property. Two thirds went to the children, one third, the family home, to the man's wife who, lacking other income, had to go to work to make a living.

Catherine Marshall LeSourd has written a small brochure telling of the hardships she faced because her husband, Peter Marshall, died without having made a will.[3] After all bills were paid, the District of Columbia awarded Catherine one third of a very modest estate; two thirds went to her son, Peter John. Because he was a minor at the time, she had to appear in probate court to be made her son's guardian. From that time until he became of age she was required to provide a detailed financial accounting of her guardianship in court each year. The account figures had to be sworn to before a notary public and a fee paid to the office of the register of deeds for the accounting.

Though you may write your own will and sign it in the presence of witnesses, it is safer to arrange to have an attorney draw it up.

A will may cost as little as $25 or as much as $1,000 or

more, depending on where you live and the complexity of your estate. A lawyer can give you a fairly accurate estimate of his fee after a preliminary discussion for which you will prepare by: (1) deciding exactly what you want in your will; (2) listing names of beneficiaries, their addresses and relationships; (3) preparing an inventory of all property, jointly or separately owned, if your attorney asks for it; (4) being able to name your executor and an alternate—persons who are well versed in business affairs.

You should concern yourself also about federal estate taxes and state inheritance taxes. Your attorney will help you save money in this area.

People customarily will all property to the surviving spouse with a provision that states what should be done in the event of a "common disaster."

Rather than specific amounts, it is well to use percentages in willing assets to beneficiaries. Who can predict what will happen in ensuing years? A retarded or handicapped child may need a greater portion than others. In such instances trusts can be established for his or her care and/or education.

A will needs a periodic review. Births, deaths, and marriages necessitate changes. So does a move to another state, where laws regarding estate disposal differ.

An attorney who has seen the headaches which result from intestacy says: "I believe the best insurance anyone can leave those he loves is a good, lawyer-drawn will, kept up to date. It's a simple act of decency, like leaving a room you've just walked out of in good order."

Annuities

In the broad sense of the word, an annuity represents any annual allowance of income. Though pensions and Social Security provide annuities, the term is customarily thought of as a specific investment from which interest and principal are allocated to the investor in periodic payments—either for life or a specific number of years.

To clarify:
* A specific sum of money becomes available at the annuity's maturity date—from which periodic payments will be made.
* To this amount are added earnings from the fund, which should be considerable if the annuity was purchased years prior to its being distributed.
* From this sum the costs of handling the fund are subtracted.
* The net figure is divided by the number of years the annuitant is expected to live. The quotient specifies the yearly payments, which generally are dispensed periodically.

Were all factors predictable, the initial sum would be exhausted at the time of last payment. But the annuitant may live longer than his life expectancy. To provide for this possibility, the paying company will, for a premium, assume the mortality risk and guarantee payments for the actual life of the annuitant.

Annuities are available in different forms:
1. An *Immediate Life Annuity* is a contract where the insurer, for a specific purchase price, pays monthly, quarterly, semiannual, or annual income during your lifetime, the payments beginning immediately.
2. A *Deferred Annuity* is one purchased with the intention that payments begin after a stated period of years or a specific time.
3. A *Period Certain Annuity* guarantees that stipulated payments be paid to you or your beneficiary for a specific period of time.
4. A *Joint Life and Survivor Annuity* is like the immediate life annuity except that payments are made during the lives of two or more annuitants and continue at the same rate or a reduced rate until the death of the last survivor.

If you haven't paid into a deferred annuity prior to your retirement, you may consider it unwise to do so at retirement, unless you have good health and adequate resources, including sufficient reserves and ready cash to meet unforeseeable emergencies. Some people, however, believe an annuity makes sense even at retirement since approximately one third of all men aged 60 can be expected to live to be 80 and one half of all women aged 60 are expected to live to be 80 or more.

According to one expert a typical annuity investor is a person who "is near retirement; lacks a large capital fund but does have other assets; doesn't like to take money risks; finds it hard not to spend available cash; above all, is in good health with a fair chance of outwitting the mortality tables."[4]

If the above paragraph describes you, you may wish to invest in an annuity that will entitle you to receive a check every month for the rest of your life.

Trusts

A trust indicates that one person holds in trust property belonging to another. A *living trust* is one effective while a person lives. A *testamentary trust* becomes effective at death. A *revocable trust* may be changed or nullified; an *irrevocable trust* cannot be changed.

Trusts, when they come into effect, are managed by a trustee—a trusted friend, a relative, the trust department of a bank, or a trust company. Trusts can be designated to benefit individuals or charitable or religious organizations. They usually are not recommended for small estates because of handling costs involved. A trustee must be paid for handling a trust. Besides the filing of individual tax returns, trust accounts must be kept, with costs charged to the trust estate.

However, the following case histories demonstrate the usefulness of trusts:

* Mr. and Mrs. Longworth, who are in their 60s and live in Arizona, have accumulated stocks and bonds from which they receive regular dividends. Besides pension and Social Security benefits they receive rent from business property and interest from municipal bonds.

The Longworths would like to spend more time traveling. Mr. Longworth no longer enjoys managing his property. Furthermore, he wonders what would happen were he suddenly to become incapacitated.

He can solve his problems by setting up a revocable trust under which his bank would take over the management of his property. Mr. Longworth could still make whatever major business decisions are necessary. Yet he wouldn't need to worry if either he or his wife were to become ill and couldn't handle their affairs.

* Samuel Martin has an aged mother whom he wishes to provide for in case he should die before she does.

He can set up a trust in his will which would provide income from his estate for his mother as long as she lives. Then when she dies, the balance of the trust could be passed to whomever he names as the beneficiary.

* Though the major portion of Tom Paul's estate will go to his wife Marci, in his will he has stated that trusts of a specified percentage should be set up for his two children, naming his bank as the trustee.

Believing the children will benefit most from receiving the trusts in stipulated amounts, he has specified that the trustee invest these trusts in annuities for periodic payments to his heirs.

Trusts are extremely flexible. Older persons may set up trusts for themselves as income beneficiaries. You, for instance, may choose to collect all income from your assets but leave the principal to future generations or to religious or charitable organizations. Or you may collect the trust's earnings and use any part of the principal you wish.

I am personally acquainted with several individuals, among them a medical doctor, a wealthy widow, and a business executive, who have established trusts from which they will receive earnings until their demise. Afterwards the principal will go to their denomination's ministries.

By establishing several trusts of this kind, a donor may be able to assist more than one ministry—church colleges, seminaries, missions, youth ministries, or women's work.

A trust in force when you die goes directly to persons you indicate—the gift is entirely separate from the probate estate.

If you think a trust will benefit you, talk to a lawyer. If you choose a bank to act as the trustee, it's advisable to allow your lawyer to draw up the proper trust agreement.

Employment

Not all of us are able to profitably invest in the stock market or in mutual funds, nor do we own huge savings from which we can draw interest. Yet we desperately need to supplement our income. Social Security was never intended to provide our full support. What options do we have?

Since the government limits the amount of money we can earn each year if we are not 72 years of age and draw Social Security, we most likely will look for part-time employment. In spite of the scarcity of full-time jobs, there appears to be little lack of those which involve part-time work. In some instances these jobs can be found in our former field of employment. A nurse, a schoolteacher, a minister, an accountant, a secretary, a clerk may have little difficulty securing limited employment.

In some instances part-time employment may be found in a field different from the one in which we worked formerly. A retired truck driver, for instance, may seek work as a guard in a large apartment complex or with some business firm.

The Federal Government has established part-time job opportunities, too. In its Foster Grandparent program persons over 60 are hired to dispense love and attention to children who are retarded or handicapped. The program now has more than 12,000 foster grandparents serving at 157 project locations in all 50 states. They work approximately 20 hours a week, at the federal minimum wage plus transportatin costs.

Green Thumb employees beautify highways, build parks, carry out conservation programs, and assist in community services.

The *Census Bureau* has at times hired retired persons, who are able to drive and read maps, as part-time interviewers.

Self-Employment

Another possibility: become your own employer; create your own job. The IRS provides a substantial tax break for self-employed persons. Check with your Social Security office for details.

Authors may do freelance writing to supplement their Social Security incomes. A retired music teacher in Northbrook, Ill., gives piano lessons to a select group of students—children and adult—who live near the retirement home where she resides. She claims the additional income enables her to maintain her car. Below are areas which may be included in the self-employed category:

arts and crafts	music instruction
interior decorating	piano tuning
home tutoring	painting
nursing	library assistance
catering	carpentry
baby-sitting	landscaping
photography	housecleaning
home secretarial work	lecturing

You may think of other areas you would like to pursue. Look into your life. Ask yourself what talent or expertise you have for which someone may be willing to pay. I assume you know that after 72 you may earn as much as you wish or are able to without any Social Security deduction.

Personal Expenditures
Food-Stamp Eligibility

Established by Congress in 1964, the food-stamp program has as its goal adequate nutrition for all

Americans. Applicants must meet nationwide standards for net income and resources, or they must have previously qualified for public assistance. Though we have seen a great amount of misuse of this program, statistics show that, among the elderly, only 28 percent of the blind and disabled persons eligible for the program participate in it. If you believe you qualify, visit your county welfare office and file an application. Take with you the following information:
* Receipts for rent or house payments; utility bills
* Proof of income
* Bank books and other proof of reserve funds
* Receipts or bills for medical care
You may find that you are eligible for this program which can be a great help to your food budget.

Low-Cost Meals

The federally sponsored Meals-on-Wheels program (not available in all localities) provides for the delivery of modestly priced, nutritious meals to elderly persons who are housebound.

In some cities senior citizen centers and churches provide similar federally subsidized meals to the mobile elderly.

Realizing older people do not eat as much food as those who are younger, some restaurants permit a couple to order and share one meal. There may be a small charge for the second table service. The cost of the second beverage must be paid for.

Discounts and Privileges

Investigate transportation discounts in your locality. In our town senior citizens may take advantage of "Dial-a-Bus" rides, for which they are charged 25 cents. The bus picks them up at their home and delivers them to their destination.

In larger cities buses charge less or no fee during nonrush periods of the day.

Many colleges offer discount tuition prices to students over 62.

During the 1975/1976 tax season 5,000 counselors, under the sponsorship of the Association of Retired Persons, helped nearly 300,000 elderly persons complete their tax returns. If such service is available in your community, you may want to take advantage of it.

Traveling? Check motels which advertise a 10% discount for elderly people.

Health Care Privileges

You cut medical expenses when you take advantage of the free flu shots and free glaucoma, diabetes, and blood pressure tests made available in most communities.

Discriminate Shopping

Watch for end-of-the-season sales. You can purchase much of your clothing at 25 to 50 percent discount at this time.

Shop markets where farmers sell produce at reduced prices.

Compare drug prices. The National Association of Retired Persons periodically lists their drug prices in their magazine, *Modern Maturity.* Both over-the-counter and prescription drugs may be purchased from them.

Act II shops exist in most large cities. Their name indicates that the clothing they sell on consignment has been worn previously—most often by persons in the upper-income bracket. If you shop wisely you may find a "Dior" at a "Levi" price.

Have you ever visited thrift shops? Besides the Salvation Army and Goodwill Industries, hospital auxiliaries, veterans groups, and Christian day schools sell used household furnishings, clothing, and appliances at a fraction of their original cost.

One day an artist stopped at a veterans' thrift shop to look for used picture frames. An expensive man's suit in her husband's size caught her eye. When she examined it, she discovered that though it carried a top-brand label it had never been worn. It's price—$13. This woman claims she has saved hundreds of dollars by purchasing, with caution, thrift-shop merchandise.

Miscellaneous Advice

 * If you enjoy gardening and have the space and energy, you can raise your own food and can or freeze it.
 * Reduce utility bills by closing doors and heating and air-conditioning vents in rooms which are not being used.
 * Bake several items at the same time.
 * Buy day-old bread.
 * Dine by candlelight
 * If you are able, walk; don't ride.
 * Join a car pool for marketing, church attendance, and social functions.
 * Take advantage of reduced telephone rates. Your children and grandchildren may live in an area where the time is 1, 2, or 3 hours later than yours. If so, call them before 8 in the morning. If they live in an area where the time is 1, 2, or 3 hours earlier than yours, place your call after 11 at night. You'll pay a fraction of the daytime rate for each call.

Frauds

Frauds have infested our society for decades. They'll continue to harrass us as long as we live, particularly during retirement. We are vulnerable to one shady deal after another when we open our mail, answer our phone, or go to our front door. Because this is true, it's advisable to learn about types of fraud that seek to ravage our retirement funds.

Land Frauds

According to one report:[5]
 * A government executive purchased a waterfront lot so he could live near his yacht. After the purchase he

learned that the canal on which the lot was located was too shallow to accommodate his boat.

* An Ohio civil servant who invested $3,600 in five acres of New Mexico land found he had bought useless property on a steep hill.

* A Canadian couple who paid $6,702 for a lot in Arizona later learned its true value—$90. They were forced to continue to make payments even though they had no hope of recovering their investment. Before filing bankruptcy, the developer sold the couple's installment contract to another firm, to which they were then obligated.

Fortunately agencies of the Federal government are striving to halt this type of fraud. Nevertheless, caution is recommended. Too many dealers still wear slyboots.

Phony Bank-Examiner Swindles

Let's pretend you are about to become a victim of this type of fraud. One day as you line up in front of a bank teller's window, a confidence man steps up behind you. By peering over your shoulder with ears and eyes alert, he learns the amount of your deposit, your account number and, because you record your balance in your checkbook, your balance as well.

Without your knowledge this man follows you to your home, learns your name and address. The next morning you receive a phone call. The man identifies himself as a bank examiner.

"I've discovered some shortages in the bank where you do business," he tells you. "The bank president tells me you are a person I can trust to help me trap one of his employees. Will you cooperate?"

"I suppose so," you answer. "What do you want me to do?"

"I'd like you to go to the bank and make a cash withdrawal of $1,000 to $2,000. One of our investigators will pick up the money at your home and redeposit it in your account together with a $500 appreciation bonus for your cooperation."

You do as you are instructed. The result? You find your account has been depleted by the con men.

According to one report, in one month two "bank-examiner" swindlers managed to steal $55,000 from elderly women in Los Angeles.

The "Pigeon Drop"

This old swindle continues to dupe people out of their savings. A woman rushes up to you saying, in essence: "I found this large sum of money and since you look like an honest person I'll share it with you if you will put up some money to show your good faith." This is done so cleverly, with the help of an accomplice who pretends not to know the first woman, that people will actually go to the bank, withdraw their savings, and give them to a total stranger, usually to a third accomplice posing as a lawyer who will divide the money that has supposedly been found.

Telephone Gyps

"Hello. This is the Blank Company. You signed for our product giveaway? Good! I have a surprise for you. You are the winner. You may call for your prize at your convenience."

At your convenience you discover your prize isn't the model you saw previously, but a very inferior product. For "just a few dollars more," you are advised, you can exchange your prize for a superior model, which more often than not is excessively overpriced.

You wouldn't fall for such a scheme? Perhaps you wouldn't, but too many people do.

Mail-Order Schemes

Many mail order schemes involve work-at-home and make-big-money deals. Address envelopes, make aprons, dolls, whatever. Beware. Usually they are come-ons where you are asked to pay additional money for instructions to do something you won't be able to find a market for.

Home-Improvement Gyps

You answer your doorbell.

"I am a city 'termite,' 'home safety,' or 'water' inspector," the man at the door tells you.

You believe him and suggest he proceed with his inspection. When it is completed you are pressured to remedy whatever wrong the man discovers—with the helpful expertise of a "most reliable" firm he recommends.

Prefinanced Funeral Plans

Unreliable prefinanced funeral packages are considered the most despicable of all money frauds, chiefly because the victim is dead when the swindle is exposed. The sellers of these plans do not deliver what they promise—casket, mortuary facilities, and a cemetery lot. If you fall for their sales pitch you may end up with only a cheap casket. Your heirs will be charged a large sum for all other services. Or they may find that by the time of your demise the purveyors of the plan are no longer in business.

Do realize, however, that some prefinanced plans are honest and reliable. If you plan to remain where you live now, such an investment may be advisable if you do business only with a firm whose reputation is flawless. Should you consider moving to another part of the country at a later date, however, a prefinanced arrangement need not concern you.

Questionable Solicitations

Unless you are well acquainted with a particular charity or religious organization and its solicitation practices, withhold your giving! Of the $10.6 billion that individuals in this country give to charities, some $10 million goes to phonies or to professional fund-raisers who absorb most of the contributions.

So give through your United Fund, the American Red

Cross, or other charities whose integrity you can trust. If in doubt, check with the Better Business Bureau. Be as diligent when it comes to religious contributions. One so-called religious promoter invites his magazine readers and his audiences to mail or give him "seed" money in $5, $10, $100 denominations with the promise that, "because God wants you to become rich, He will reward you with greater wealth than you have ever dreamed possible."

If you wish to supplement your church contributions by giving to some other religious endeavor, don't hesitate to ask for a financial statement. One woman said that when she was going to make her will she wrote to several religious organizations asking to see their financial statement. Only one director complied. She gave her contribution to his organization. Reliable organizations do not hide their business practices.

4

Hobbies
and Second Careers

"I dread the thought of retirement," a man about to leave his position as superintendent of a small-town school told me one day. "I'm a regimented person. I shift gears according to fixed schedules.

"Some of my friends have retired to a life of fun and games. Sure, I like golf, but not like meals in a day. I keep wondering what I'll do to fill my time."

A mutual friend countered, "I'm looking forward to retirement. I'll have time to pursue my hobbies, go back to school, whatever."

These two people look at retirement through different-angled lenses. The school superintendent dreads what he assumes will be a nonscheduled, boring existence of endless leisure, while our mutual friend anticipates a creative future.

Maintaining Routine

The school superintendent should realize he need not forfeit routine in retirement. In fact, a certain amount of routine ought always be maintained. I suggest he:

* Keep regular hours. Begin the day by rising when he normally does.

* Start a project and keep at it until it is completed. He can make a list of books he wishes to read, then read them. Let's say he decides to read the entire Bible through in a year's time. A portion of each day will be given to this activity. Or he can do something to improve his living

46

quarters, learn a new language, take college courses in which he has always been interested but never had time to pursue.

* Set aside specific time of the day for a brisk walk. Invite his spouse or a friend to accompany him.

These activities, though they suggest discipline and routine, also represent leisure pursuits. But the superintendent need not fear them.

Swiss psychologist/theologian Paul Tournier explains why the thought of retirement frightens so many of us.[1] Trained to work and to keep busy, we have been conditioned to feel guilty if we indulge in leisure activity. We sit down to read a book, watch television, or play a game of chess feeling that "really now, I ought not take the time."

Dr. Tournier urges persons approaching retirement to plan and learn how to enjoy leisure-time activities. So, read that book, take up some hobby, play that game of chess. Relax and begin now.

Hobbies and Leisure Pursuits

The retirement world is full of persons who have taken Dr. Tournier's advice. They say, "I wish my days were twice as long. I just don't have time to do all I'd like to do."

Harold Dye, who wrote the book *No Rocking Chair for Me,*[2] tells about a "Rockathon" described in the *Guinness Book of Records*. The winner, Ralph Wier of Truro, N. S., set a world record by rocking for 106 hours. Of the event Mr. Dye says, "The man had been nowhere at all." Mr. Dye looked forward to a retirement life which would take him somewhere. That somewhere involved the building of a retirement home and the pursuit of a number of hobbies including backpacking, hunting, and fishing.

Those who say their days aren't long enough continue being creative as long as they live. Artists Renoir, Matisse, and Picasso must have vowed they would paint as long as they could hold a brush. In painting they continued to express their creative genius. Or take Grandma Moses as

47

an example. Though she began painting in her 70s, she had painted more than 1,000 primitives and made herself world famous by the time she celebrated her 100th birthday in 1961.

When in her 80s, Mildred Comfort, a St. Paul, Minn., author, wrote two biographies for teenagers each year.

A 1975 article describes Edna Gardner White as having "her head in the clouds." At 72 this owner and operator of the Aero Valley Estates Airport in Roanoke, Tex., flew three to seven hours a day. During her aviation years she trained close to 4,000 flying students.

Under the leadership of Karl Oldberg, a group of retirees in Southern California organized the *Southland Courtwatchers,* whose members visit and follow court hearings. While they don't attempt to evaluate the court, lawyers, and judges in each trial, they do, in panel discussions of their own, try to come up with a verdict which may or may not coincide with that of the jury.

Other retirees fish, hunt, or backpack into wilderness country. Many take extended trips sponsored by travel agencies, church or fraternal organizations, or by the American Association of Retired Persons. Some take mini trips to points of interest.

Be Yourself

In a wide range of activities, rug hooking, oil painting, china painting, gem cutting, ceramics, gardening—whatever it may be—do realize that inner fulfillment and improvement are more important than perfection. Inner fulfillment will come through the choice of a pursuit in which you are vitally interested and for which you possess special talent. Don't let anyone pressure you into pursuing a hobby or activity which doesn't suit you. Your hobby, your leisure activity, should reflect your personality—not someone else's.

I think of one of Ralph Seager's poems in this connection:

I cannot sing another's song

For him so right, for me so wrong.
I'll make my own come clean and fine,
The chances are he can't sing mine.[3]

I recall a business executive who took up photography after his retirement. He attended some college classes in photography, fashioned a darkroom in his basement. Eventually he became so proficient that he teamed up with his wife, an author. When she wrote an article, he took the pictures which illustrated it. Photography was his thing, writing hers.

One of my husband's aunts, a fine seamstress, decided to sew for other people after her husband passed away. Visiting her when she was 80, we learned she had just completed a wedding dress and bridesmaids' gowns for an upcoming local wedding. A sister who lived with her said, "I don't know how she does it. I couldn't."

Of course she couldn't. She wasn't interested in, nor did she possess dressmaking skill.

Do realize, however, that there may be others in your community who are interested in the same activities and possess the same talents you do. Many cities have chess clubs, oil, ceramic, and china painting groups, stamp and coin colectors' organizations, writers' clubs—whatever—where inspiration and ideas can be shared for the benefit of all.

Library Assistance

Libraries, too, can assist you in cultivating retirement activities, one of which may be reading.

Browsing in a library recently, I accidentally bumped into a friend whose arms were laden with several "Great Books" texts. "Going to lead a Great Books discussion session?" I asked.

"Nope," he answered. "I'm going to wade through these books alone. It's something I promised myself a long time ago."

Have you visited your library recently? If you haven't, you will be surprised at what it has to offer. Besides books (many in large print) you'll find current magazines, newspapers, microfilm materials, phonograph records, tape recordings, slides, films, sheet music, and much more. You can even borrow framed artwork to hang on the walls of your home for a specific period of time. Some libraries have bookmobiles which take books to areas that do not have a library. Others offer library services to home shut-ins and hospital patients. Did you know the library also makes available a number of large-city telephone directories?

The best way to get acquainted with your library is to browse through it for a few hours. Learn where the things I have mentioned are located. Librarians are among the most helpful people in the world. Don't hesitate to ask for assistance when you need it.

Back to School

The increased use of library facilities indicates that many retired persons are interested in stretching their minds, either for their own personal fulfillment or as a stepping stone to a second career.

More than 500 institutions in the U. S. are now offering special courses and services for older persons. Georgia Southern College at Statesboro not only has a Center for Continuing Education but, in cooperation with the State Extension Service, presents seminars for older persons. At Syracuse University 400 residents of a public housing project on the campus share full use of university facilities. In Iowa 600 older persons in a large rural area near Waterloo take classes of the Hawkeye Institution of Technology at different campus locations.

In most cities adult education classes offer courses in gourmet cooking, oil painting, photography, upholstery, real estate, computer education, interior decorating, hospital-aid services—any one of which could be adapted to a second career.

A refresher course in typing may lead to part-time secretarial work; a thorough study of a particular country may qualify you for a position as a tour guide. If you can produce good artwork, be it oil paintings, ceramic, pottery, or china painting, you may be able to sell your work for profit or, for a fee, teach others the art skills you have mastered.

Perhaps you'd like to try your hand at free-lance writing. Enroll in local college or adult education creative writing courses. Attend writers conferences in your area. There you will meet other writers, beginners and pros, as well as editors who may be looking for the type of material you are able to produce.

If you are a retired minister, you may wish to apply for a position as visitation pastor in some church or as a chaplain for a group of nursing homes.

In such second-career involvement you can control and limit the number of hours you work. Don't force yourself to do more than you are able to—and do only what you most enjoy! Retirement is the time when you have that option.

The Worth of an Older Worker

If you have special training and skill, don't let your age hinder you from applying for a job you want. Statistics prove that workers 65 or older hold their own beside younger workers. An over-65 uncle worked side by side with his much-younger nephew in the roofing business with no significant difference in the quality of their work.

A U. S. Department of Labor Survey compares younger and older workers as to:

* Productivity: Output per man-hour shows no significant decline until after 55, and then only a small drop. Many older workers exceed the average output of younger age groups.

* Stability: Older workers are not job-hoppers. They stay on a job for longer periods of time than younger workers—an important quality when the employer is considering the cost of turnover.

* Absenteeism: Older workers, including women, do not take as much time off from a job as younger workers.

Their willingness to work does not drop as they pass middle age.

* Skill: Older job-seekers offer longer work experience plus higher skills. Yet they usually constitute more than half of the reservoir of unemployed skilled workers.

* Adaptability: Older workers show considerable flexibility in adapting to job situations.[4]

So if you want to go back to work, you should make every effort to find the job you like and can do. In applying for a particular job, point out the above advantages of hiring an older person. Don't be too modest. Make the most of your assets. After all, it is you who make retirement boring or full of promise.

5

Help Yourself
by Helping Others

Though hobbies and second careers do add interest and
significance to one's life, they can be overdone. An added
ingredient is needed—meaningful involvement in other
people's lives, as the following story aptly illustrates.

At 75, prior to the inauguration of the federal
government's "Foster-Grandparent" program, George
Dennowith launched a "grandparent" career of his own.

He had heard a great deal about the Cambridge, Minn.,
home for retarded persons, 15 miles from his home. One
day he decided to visit the institution. When he entered the
building he joined a tour group composed of five women,
each of whom had come to "adopt" a needy child. In
mental-institution parlance this means they would select a
child with whom they could visit and on whom they could
bestow tender loving care.

As they made their way to the children's wards, Mr.
Dennowith felt great pity for the old and the young who
were unable to care for themselves.

Upon entering one ward, he stayed by the entrance
door while the women spoke to an attendant about the
purpose of their visit.

Suddenly a small, emaciated boy spied him. As fast as
he could maneuver his little body on his hands and knees,
he crawled across the room. Then reaching up he put his
arms around Mr. Dennowith's legs.

The attendant gasped. "Why I never!" she began.
"That child hasn't once paid the slightest attention to

anyone who has come into this room. I just can't understand it."

"I can," one of the women countered. Turning to Mr. Dennowith, she said, "Mister, you've found your child. No, that's not right. That child found you."

Mr. Dennowith looked at the boy who clung to his legs and stared at him with eyes devoid of expression. So different from the alert, intelligent look of his own grandchildren when they were young, he thought. But how could he, an old man, help this child? On the other hand, how could he not help him? He had the time, he possessed good health, and he did love children. What more could he ask?

So before he left the building he had promised to make periodic visits to this 7-year-old mongoloid child named Martin.

His first efforts to help him proved discouraging. Mr. Dennowith tried to get the boy to stand on his feet. He refused. Instead he crawled across the room to a chair and, raising himself slowly, began to pound and claw at it with his hands.

But Mr. Dennowith didn't give up. With infinite patience he brought about a great change in the child. "At first I wondered if I could," he said. "Martin never cried. In fact, he made no sound at all. Then a miracle happened. One morning Martin smiled! I'll never forget that smile."

Mr. Dennowith requisitioned shoes for the boy, and after many tedious hours taught him to stand on his feet, then to walk short distances. Eventually the boy was able to take his "grandfather's" hand and walk by his side. He also learned to stoop and pick up objects on the floor in front of him and to feed himself.

When I think of Mr. Dennowith, I recall a statement I heard a speaker quote: "I've never seen a hypochondriac who wasn't a bore; conversely, I've never seen a person concerned about others who was a hypochondriac."

Mr. Dennowith's story and similar stories by other foster grandparents help us understand that though hobbies and second careers have great merit, volunteer involvement—the giving of ourselves to others—represents in-depth, meaningful living that transcends all other activities.

Are you ever lonely, bored, or depressed? You needn't be if you regularly volunteer a portion of your time to some person, institution, or cause. If you possess good health, you enjoy the necessary energy for such involvement. If you aren't as hale as you would like to be, the giving of yourself to others may help you forget your own problems. Your spirit will be renewed, your introspection reversed.

A Wide-Open Door

You may choose to begin this type of involvement in your own neighborhood and community. In this era of transient living a great many families are separated from their kin—children from parents, grandchildren from grandparents. You can assume a grandparent role for such a family. Perhaps a young mother needs someone to baby-sit her small children while she visits her doctor or dentist, shops, or attends a parent-teacher counseling session.

One day shortly after we had moved to a parish in Duluth, Minn., an elderly parishioner called asking if she could baby-sit our children.

"I don't want any pay," she told me. "It's just that I get terribly lonely. Please call me whenever you need me."

I learned to love this woman as much as my children did. She freed me to assume church responsibilities I could not have undertaken without her help. Reading, playing games, whatever, she became a surrogate grandmother to our children.

Local "well-baby" clinics, sponsored by county health associations, need nurse assistants during medical examinations and special care procedures. They also need baby-sitters for children who must accompany their mothers who bring their infants to the clinic.

Think, too, of nursing home and hospital needs for volunteers. You can lend a listening ear, write letters, shop for nursing home residents. In some instances you may feed the patients who cannot feed themselves. Hospitals constantly depend on volunteers to assist in the admittance and dismissal of patients, in the distribution of mail, flowers, and library books.

For several years Ruth Chorley, a retired artist/schoolteacher, served as a volunteer speech therapist for stroke patients in a nursing home near her apartment. "It's the most rewarding work I've done," she claims.

Lucille Gates, Phoenix, Ariz., chauffeurs cancer patients who must make periodic visits to local medical centers for treatment and care.

A great many elderly people live under a pall of loneliness. Some become so starved for some type of communication they cut and mail in coupons from magazine advertisements. This assures them of a response.

Several years ago a Christian psychologist, Dr. Karl T. Waugh, developed what he called the "League of the Golden Pen" in one of his classes at Beloit College. He urged his students to write a least one letter a week to someone with whom they were not presently corresponding. "Or pick a name from the phone book," he told them.

You can appropriate Dr. Waugh's plan. Perhaps there is someone in your past to whom you owe a debt of gratitude. Recently a friend reminded me of a high school teacher who had taught us to love words and their proper use. Realizing I had never thanked this teacher, I sat down and wrote her a letter of appreciation. I should have done so sooner.

A friend who lost a small child in a tractor accident writes letters of condolence to families she learns have gone through a similar experience.

A little brainstorming on your part will enable you to recall names of persons who would be delighted to hear from you. Think especially of the elderly who are lonely.

Have you considered offering to deliver Meals-on-Wheels to shut-ins or assisting in serving meals to the mobile elderly at church and senior-citizen centers? Have you considered becoming active in the telephone-assurance program, which requires that you call elderly persons assigned to you to learn if they are well or if they are in need of special help?

In the city where I live a group of retired persons have organized a food-distribution program. They collect and bag produce provided by ranchers and merchants, and canned goods from nearby canneries. An identification card which costs one dollar entitles the owner to a large shopping bag of food (fresh corn, carrots, sweet potatoes, grapes, melons, canned fruit, whatever is currently available) each week.

A retired friend, Josephine Nelson, St. Paul, Minn., helps prepare book recordings for the blind. Others read textbooks to blind college students.

If you wish a complete change of scene when you retire, you might consider spending two or more years in a needy country as a member of the Peace Corps sharing your expertise, whether it be as an agronomist, engineer, builder, medical specialist, or teacher. You might also consider serving people in an area of extreme poverty in this country as a member of our "domestic Peace Corps," VISTA (Volunteers in Service to America). Neither program has set an upper age limit for volunteers. Both make it possible for husbands and wives to work together. Even persons in their 80s have found fulfillment in this type of service.

Or you may participate in RSVP (Retired Senior Volunteer Program), a new federally aided, community-based volunteer program designed to give retirees an opportunity for person-to-person service.

Remember Your Church

Some retirees serve their local churches, their district conferences, or their mission boards on a volunteer basis.

Upon retirement, Ernest Hanson, a department super-visor at New Departure, a division of General Motors in

Bristol, Conn., became his pastor's assistant. He handled all clerical tasks, prepared a weekly newsletter, the church bulletin, and the church's annual reports.

Alvin Oberg, a Southern Pacific Railroad executive, served his denomination's Southwest conference gratis, as a treasurer, for 10 years following his retirement.

Ada Whiting, a retired city librarian, helped establish and operate one of the finest church libraries in the country.

Many people visit shut-in members of their church, or nursing-home residents, regularly. One woman has established a tape ministry in a number of nursing homes. Each week she plays a sermon and music tapes for those who are interested.

Numerous persons have offered clerical, technical, and educational assistance to foreign missionary organizations on a short-term basis. Janet Peterson spent a year as bookkeeper at a missionary radio station in Nome, Alaska.

Even your reading can help others. In one eastern city a group of church members who liked to read met once a month to discuss a current religious book. Prior to the meeting each person purchased the book the group chose to study. Following the discussion of the book, members mailed their copies to missionary friends abroad.

If you have musical talent, share it with your church. A word of warning, however. Don't hang onto a job as choir director, church organist, soloist, or whatever, so long that the church is placed in the embarrassing position of having to ask you to step aside. Remember the younger musicians who need to develop their talent.

But, and I underscore the word, you don't need to be shelved. Organize and direct a senior-citizens' choir, male chorus, or orchestra. Or offer to give piano, organ, or other instrumental lessons to young people who cannot afford them.

Remember, too, that your church needs your prayers. In the quietness of your home you strengthen your own spiritual life when you meditate on God's Word and when you commune with Him in prayer.

In some churches members are placed in prayer groups of four or five. Each participant receives a notice each month informing him of those in his group for whom he is to pray. Individuals often call their prayer-partners when they have special burdens and needs.

Pray for your pastor, the church officers, church-school personnel, church musicians, the custodian, the ushers. Extend your prayer concern to your denomination's leaders, board members, and publication personnel. Have you ever prayed for the editor of your church publications? Have your prayed for the writers who contribute material to them? Pray also for missionaries.

Then, pray for yourself. As a rule we busy ourselves with so many activities we don't have time to sit quietly and bask in the love of God.

There seems to be a special need for such quietness—note the popularity of meditation groups today. Participants of one particular group are given a "mantra," a secret, usually meaningless word, on which to focus their attention as they meditate.

Why shouldn't we have our own mantras? A speaker recently suggested the doxology: "GLORY BE TO THE FATHER, AND TO THE SON, AND TO THE HOLY SPIRIT. AS IT WAS IN THE BEGINNING, IS NOW, AND SHALL EVER BE, WORLD WITHOUT END. AMEN."

Or it can be a portion of Scripture or a favorite hymn—Psalm 103 or the hymn "How Great Thou Art!"

Ask God to give you direction in choosing the volunteer work where you would be most effective. The Bible says, "In all thy ways acknowledge Him, and He shall direct thy paths" (Proverbs 3:6).

We become better persons when we pray. As better persons we serve God and others more effectively.

Occasionally you may find you cannot verbalize a prayer to God. On those occasions you may choose to read prayers written by other people. I especially enjoy the prayers of John Baillie.[1] In some instances he has left blank spaces where you can insert the names of people for whom you wish to pray that particular prayer.

You help others, too, by listening. Can you keep a confidence? Are you understanding? Can you empathize with other people's problems? Then share your time with those who have special struggles. Recently a young pastor's wife from another denomination called me about a problem. When I had listened to her story and tried to help her solve it, she said, "I don't have anyone else to whom I can go." I am glad she thought enough of me to confide in me this way.

Get Youth Involved

As valuable as your own assistance is the interest you can instill in others, especially in the youth, to do volunteer work. Nursing-home patients rarely see young people and children. They appreciate visits from them.

Charlene and David Myhre have made a Jewish nursing home their personal responsibility. Often they take children with them to visit with or sing for the elderly.

In preparation for one visit they asked the children if they would like to "adopt" one of the residents as their grandparent. They didn't force the children, just asked them to volunteer if they wanted to.

One by one, the children asked different residents if they would be grandmother or grandfather to them. One small child, seven or eight, hesitated. But just as the group was ready to leave the building she turned to Charlene and said, "Will you go with me? I want to ask Mrs. Cohen to be my grandmother."

Charlene took the girl to the woman's room. "Mrs. Cohen, could . . . could," she stammered, nervously twisting a lock of her hair. "Could I be your grandmother?"

Mrs. Cohen laughed heartily. "You surely could," she

answered. Then, winking at the girl, added, "But maybe it would be better if I became your grandmother."

For many weeks the residents of the nursing home spoke warmly of the incident.

The Crux of the Matter

In one of his *Power* magazine columns[2] Henry Jacobson, Sun City, Ariz., claims the village's retirees often say, "I'm busier now than I've ever been."

When he asks what they are busy at, they reel off a list of recreational activities—golf, swimming, bowling, travel, shuffleboard, ceramics. . . .

Jacobson says, "Of course it is far better to be occupied with enjoyable, healthful recreational activities than to sit and simmer for lack of things to do. But it seems to me these retired persons, especially the Christians, ought to ask themselves once in awhile if God doesn't expect them to devote some of their time to His service."

And what is *His* service?

One day after speaking of the Christians' need to help others, Jesus said, "Inasmuch as ye have done it unto one of the least of these My brethren, ye have done it unto Me" (Matthew 25:40).

6

Health Is Wealth

To guard is better than to heal,—
The shield is nobler than the spear.
Oliver Wendell Holmes

In retirement you will be as concerned about your health as you are about any of the other problems you or a loved one may face as you grow old.

For many years medics focused their attention almost entirely on the care of patients and the relief of their suffering. Later, thanks to bioscience and technology, physicians shifted their concern to saving lives. Which is as it should be. When we become ill we desire more than anything that our doctor strives to restore our health as quickly and completely as possible.

But, as we may allow the above quotation to imply, guarding health may be nobler than restoring it. How fortunate, then, that researchers learned to isolate the germs that cause infectious diseases and to perfect the immunization that prevents them!

Note how successful they have been. At the turn of the century infectious diseases topped the list of the 10 leading causes of death in the United States. By 1960 only influenza and pneumonia, which had ranked first, remained on the list.

Today heart disease, cancer, and strokes kill most frequently. Accidents, influenza, and pneumonia, diseases of infancy, diabetes, cirrhosis of the liver, and emphysema complete the list of the 10 leading causes of death in the United States.[1]

Though the late Dr. Edward J. Sieglitz, well-know

62

geriatric specialist, applauded preventive procedures, he declared they cannot be considered the sole responsibility of the medical profession. Good health, he said, is not a fundamental right but a privilege which must be accepted as the personal responsibility of every individual.[2]

To be able to accept such responsibility we need to understand the nature and the treatment of diseases which may play havoc with our health as we age.

Cardiovascular Diseases

Hypertension

A word often incorrectly used to indicate tension or anxiety, hypertension is the medical term for high blood pressure.

Large as a man's fist, your heart daily forces 10 tons of blood through your body. Each time it beats, this force or pressure increases; each time it relaxes, the pressure decreases.

When your doctor checks your blood pressure, he measures how high an artery's blood pressure can raise a column of mercury in a glass tube. He records the measurement as one would a fraction, say 120/80, which is considered ideal, though readings slightly above or below this level may be considered safe. The 120 represents the systolic pressure, the amount of force exerted when the heart contracts and pushes blood through the body. The 80 represents the diastolic pressure, the resistance in the circulatory system at all times and the more significant figure to consider as a factor in many cardiovascular diseases.

If your blood pressure exceeds the norm by as much as 140/90 or 140/95, your doctor will prescribe medication and, as likely, a diet (to help you lose weight or to decrease your intake of salt) that will reduce your pressure and keep it under control.

It is estimated that one of every seven adults (one of five over 55) has hypertension. At least 11 million are unaware of their problem. High blood pressure, which causes 60,000 deaths a year, is also the major factor in a million deaths where strokes and cardiovascular disorders are involved.[3] Recent studies indicate that even a slight elevation many cause health problems.

If you have never concerned yourself about hypertension, realize that no one is immune. Your blood pressure can rise without warning. That's one reason why medical checkups should be scheduled once a year. A warning: Be sure the blood pressure is taken by a professional, a qualified nurse or a doctor.

Arteriosclerosis

Known also as hardening of the arteries, arteriosclerosis covers a variety of conditions that cause the artery walls to thicken and become hard, thus losing their elasticity. Atherosclerosis, a form of arteriosclerosis, represents a condition where fatty deposits and calcium clog artery channels.

Though doctors speak cautiously about "cures" they believe arteriosclerosis can be slowed, in some cases reversed, by reaming of the arteries. Because individuals with arteriosclerosis have a high level of cholesterol, the fatlike substance in the blood, they are advised to curtail, sometimes eliminate, saturated-fat products such as milk, eggs, butter, and fatty meats from their diets. A high level of triglycerides, another fatty substance, prompts doctors to limit the intake of carbohydrates and starches— desserts, candy, potatoes.

Studies which compared the Bantu African and Japanese low-fat diets with the high-animal-fat diets of the Europeans and North Americans indicated a greater incidence of atherosclerosis in the latter group.[4]

Dr. Hugh Trowell of England, formerly consultant physician to the Ugandan government, found that rural Africans who ate foods rich in fiber have low blood-cholesterol levels.

In one study where the addition of butter increased the cholesterol levels, foods high in fiber content caused it to drop as much as 20 percent.[5] This may be the reason why some doctors recommend breakfast diets which include a bowl of whole bran.

Coronary Thrombosis

When atherosclerosis attacks, artery walls narrow, causing blood to coagulate and form a clot (a thrombus) which obstructs the blood flow. The bloodstream may carry the clot to other parts of the body. Then the affected tissue starves for lack of life-sustaining oxygen.

When this occlusion robs the heart of needed oxygen, it can no longer function properly. We call this type of occlusion a *heart attack*. Physicians label it a *coronary thrombosis*, a *coronary occlusion*, or a *myocardial infarction*.

The mildness or severity of a heart attack depends on the location of the blood stoppage. If the interference occurs in the main trunk of one of the coronary arteries which send nourishment to the heart, greater damage will result than if it occurs in one of the smaller branches leading from the heart.

Though you may experience a heart attack without knowing it, most often an attack occurs with devastating intensity. Excruciating pain would strike the center of your chest and radiate through your left arm, shoulder, neck, and jaw. Because of curtailed oxygen you would feel as though you couldn't breathe. You would pale, become nauseated and weak. You might lose consciousness.

If the pain persists, grab a phone and call your doctor. Better yet call an ambulance, the fire or police department. The object is to get to the hospital as speedily as possible.

Upon arrival insist that you receive immediate attention. Time is never so precious as it is during the first minutes and hours following a heart attack.

No doubt oxygen will be administered. Your doctor will prescribe a drug that delays clotting, one that expands artery walls, as well as medication which kills pain and helps you relax.

Angina Pectoris

Angina pectoris describes a heart condition which more often affects older than younger persons. It is not a heart attack in the same sense as a coronary thrombosis is, though it can be attributed to the same cause. The difference lies in the fact that a reduced amount of blood continues to reach the heart. This reduction is usually temporary.

Angina can be caused by emotional stress or overexertion—walking, running, or shoveling snow. Weeks, even months, may elapse between attacks.

Nonaddicting nitroglycerine tablets placed under the tongue provide quick relief from angina pain. They dilate coronary blood vessels so that more oxygen-carrying blood can reach the heart muscle.

Should you be angina-prone, make sure you always have a fresh supply of nitroglycerine tablets on hand, in a bottle with a cap you can open speedily with ease. Avoid overexertion, intense cold or heat, and emotional upsets. Refrain from smoking and follow the diet your doctor prescribes.

Congestive Heart Failure

Congestive heart failure occurs when the heart's ability to pump blood has been curtailed either by diseases of the circulatory system or by damage to the heart structure.

When the heart cannot maintain satisfactory circulation in the body, blood backs up in the veins, causing congestion in the body tissues. Fluid accumulates, particularly in the legs and ankles, and breathing becomes labored.

Congestive heart failure requires rest as well as drugs which eliminate fluid. Digitalis is usually prescribed to strengthen heart muscles.

Strokes (Apoplexy)

Strokes, cerebral vascular accidents, occur in older

persons who have hardening of the arteries or other blood diseases. A brain vessel that has lost its elasticity breaks as a result of suddenly increased blood pressure, extreme physical exertion, or emotional stress. A blood clot in the brain may also cause a stroke. In either instance paralysis in varying degrees strikes one side of the body, one leg and arm and one side of the face. A victim may lose consciousness.

The severity or mildness of a stroke is determined by the size of the broken blood vessel or clot and its location in the brain. Though apoplexy may be fatal, often lost mobility can be restored by medication and therapy.

We know now that certain types of strokes can be postponed, in some cases prevented altogether. Your responsibility involves checking your blood pressure periodically, reducing emotional stress, and watching for stroke warnings: numbness of the hands and face, eyesight problems, dizziness, acute headaches, slurred speech.

Though most cardiovascular diseases do not require surgery, in some cases it becomes mandatory. Heart surgeons clean out or replace clogged blood vessels. In a "coronary bypass" they take veins from another part of the body (usually the leg) and use them to bypass the clogged or malfunctioning heart vessels. No doubt you know several persons who are alive today because they underwent a coronary bypass.

In other operations doctors replace diseased heart valves. They also implant pacemakers in the body, thus providing electric stimulation to make a sluggish heart beat as regularly as it should.

If we assess the causes of cardiovascular diseases, we understand why doctors keep repeating: "Take every measure to keep your blood pressure at its normal level. Reduce intake of saturated-fat foods. Eat whole grain cereals. Quit smoking. Exercise (walking is most profitable) as regularly and as extensively as your health permits. Relax; slow down!

Other Health Problems
Cancer

Cancer, one of man's most dreaded diseases, involves irrational, puposeless growth of cells. No respecter of persons, it invades any home, attacks any age. If you are the daughter, son, parent, spouse, or sibling of a cancer victim, you have learned the difference between benign (noncancerous) growths and malignant (cancerous) growths. A benign tumor does not invade neighboring tissues. Once removed it isn't likely to grow again. A malignant tumor, on the other hand, invades other tissues. By compression it shuts off the blood supply and destroys them. In a process known as metastasis cancer may establish growths far removed from the original cancer cells.

Though no one can pinpoint one known cause of cancer, certain chemical compounds (aniline dyes, arsenic, asbestos, benzol, pitch and tar) appear dangerous. Excessive use of X-rays and radioactive materials are known to cause leukemia and cancers of the bone, lungs, and skin. Since 1960 the U. S. Health Service has been warning that cigarette smoking causes cancer of the lungs as well as cancers of the mouth, larnyx, esophagus, and urinary bladder.

Cancer may be treated by surgery, radiation, or chemotherapy. Statistics indicate that a very high percentage of cancers, particularly of certain types, can be cured if detected and properly treated *in time.*

Should cancer strike, make sure that you secure reliable medical attention. Beware of quacks, some of whom may even have an M. D. degree. When you hear a variety of "cure" testimonies and a denunciation of the American Medical Association for its jealous bias, remember the medical profession has acknowledged hundreds of scientifically tested and proven discoveries, such as the Salk vaccine for polio.

Since speedy diagnosis is of utmost importance, you need to be alert to cancer warnings: unusual bleeding or discharge, a lump or thickening in the breast or other parts of the body, a change in normal bladder or bowel functions, a sore which refuses to heal, continuous hoarseness, persistent indigestion, difficulty in swallowing, a change in the size or color of a mole.

Diabetes

Diabetes describes a condition where abnormal amounts of sugar are discovered in the blood and urine. It indicates a failure on the part of the pancreas to produce enough insulin to allow the blood to store and properly utilize the sugar in food. The excess sugar accumulates in the blood. Some finds its way to the kidneys, where it is spilled off in the urine.

Abnormal thirst, the passage of large amounts of urine, obesity, loss of strength, and in some cases loss of weight, may indicate the presence of diabetes. There are instances, however, where victims of the disease either didn't understand these symptoms or ignored them. When an elderly easterner visited relatives in California, he suddenly became very ill, lapsed into a diabetic coma, and died. He had never complained of any diabetic symptoms to his family. In another instance an overweight man in his 60s learned that he was diabetic in a routine medical examination.

Be aware that diabetes cannot be cured. Almost all cases, however, can be controlled by insulin injections and low-sugar diets. Mild cases, known as "borderline," can be controlled by diet alone, particularly when the diabetic is elderly. By following his diet the overweight man lost weight, lowered his blood pressure, and brought his blood sugar within normal range.

Unfortunately neither diet nor medication prevent impairment of circulation in the limbs caused by atherosclerosis which is aggravated by diabetes and which, if not treated properly, could precipitate an amputation.

You may be able to forestall diabetes by keeping your

weight down, exercising, and by monitoring your intake of starches and sugar.

Arthritis

The number-one crippler, arthritis affects 11 million people in our country. It is detected when joints become inflamed and when they ache, swell, and pain in motion. In seven out of ten cases, early diagnosis and care can prevent crippling. Acute arthritis usually affects the tissue around the joints; chronic arthritis affects the bones themselves.

Osteoarthritis results from wear and tear on the joints. Many elderly people with osteoarthritis experience painful knees, backs, and fingers. Heat, braces, aspirin, cortisone injections, and other drugs may be used to relieve pain.

Rheumatic arthritis, which may attack any age, cripples most severely. Progressive, it causes joints to swell and pain, eventually to stiffen and deform. Fever, muscle weakness, and weight loss are common.

Though no miracle drug has been discovered to conquer arthritis, aspirin (the leading arthritis medication), gold injections, cortisone, and other drugs are prescribed to alleviate pain. Be aware, however, that some of these drugs may cause side effects.

For some time surgery has repaired deformed feet and hands. Today an increasing number of people (Eugene Ormandy, orchestra conductor, at 73; Margaret Chase Smith, U. S. Senator, during her 60s) have submitted to operations which replace hip joints with amazing results. Others have had operations which repair knee joints.

Following hip surgery, one woman who walked for the first time in years exclaimed, "The pain is gone. It's like being given a second life!"

Emphysema

According to expert estimates, more than a million persons (more men than women) in the U. S. suffer from emphysema, a disease which causes lungs to lose their elasticity and their ability to exhale all the carbon dioxide they should. The carbon dioxide steals space that should be replaced with fresh air, causing patients to gasp for breath as they strive to get needed oxygen into their lungs. When the disease persists, the tiny air sacs (aveoli) inflate like balloons and burst. Complications may lead to death.

Doctors believe smoking and possibly air pollution cause emphysema. In an article published in the *Turlock Journal* (November 1969) Dr. Robert Julien, Turlock, Calif., wrote: "My father, also a doctor, smoked two or three packs of cigarettes a day for thirty-five or forty years. As a result he went through all the stages of emphysema, none of which were pleasant. Though he stopped smoking five years before he died, he had to give up his practice several years prior to that time.

"He often warned me about smoking. He needn't have. As a small boy I was often awakened as he coughed and struggled to breathe. Right then I vowed I'd never smoke."

Eye Diseases

Family Health reports that approximately two million Americans have *glaucoma* and don't know it.

Though there are 45 different "glaucomas," all have one thing in common—the drainage of fluid from inside the eye is impaired and pressure builds up as it does when a balloon is inflated. The abnormal pressure curtails blood supply, causing damage to the peripheral nerves. The result: "tunnel vision," impairment of side-sight. Untreated glaucoma will eventually cause blindness.

One in every ten persons over 65 can be considered a glaucoma suspect. The most susceptible are persons who have heart ailments, diabetes, or high blood pressure.

Whether or not you suspect glaucoma, you should have your eyes examined periodically, for treatment must begin in the early stages of the disease. In testing your eyes for glaucoma the doctor will drop a small amount of local anesthetic into each eye to prevent irritation. Then as you lean back he will place the tip of a small, pressure-sensitive device called a totometer against the front of each eye. A tiny gauge on the end of the instrument will register any increase in pressure.

If your doctor diagnoses glaucoma, he will prescribe eye drops, which you must use with conscientious regularity if you expect the disease to be controlled.

"I always tell a glaucoma patient to avoid emotional stress and to quit smoking if he smokes," a prominent ophthalmologist says.

An acute form of glaucoma, acute angle-closure glaucoma, does not respond to drugs. It can be treated surgically, however. This type of glaucoma strikes suddenly with more dramatic symptoms: pain, nausea, vomiting, redness of the eyes, and dilated pupils.

Cataracts

The lens of a normal eye is a transparent, pale yellow protein located behind the colored iris. Flexible, it automatically adjusts to focus images on the retina. When the lens clouds and obstructs light, you can suspect you have cataracts.

At present surgery is the only remedy. Each year a large number of elderly persons have diseased lenses removed. After surgery corrective lenses (eyeglasses or contact lenses) are prescribed to compensate for the loss of the natural lens.

Hearing Problems

Many older persons, one of eight aged 65 to 74, one in four 75 or over, suffer some form of hearing loss. This is often the result of damage to nerve cells in the inner ear and to the nerve fibers. However, other factors may be to blame: disease, infections, exposure to loud noise, and injuries.

Whatever the cause, you need not resign yourself to deafness. An audiologist will indicate whether your hearing can be improved by treatment, by surgery, or by the use of a hearing aid.

In making your selection of a hearing aid, ask your doctor to suggest a reliable firm where the type you need can be purchased. Having investigated fraud in this area, the Federal Trade Commission recommends that, after a written recommendation by a physician or audiologist, consumers be permitted a 30-day trial period. If found unsatisfactory, the hearing aid could be returned and the buyer's money refunded. A warning: Choose with care. Then wear unashamedly as you would glasses.

To protect your hearing, have it tested regularly with an audiometer. Keep your ears clean (without the help of a sharp instrument). A doctor may need to clean out accumulated wax. A home economist who thought she had suddenly become deaf while traveling in Mexico discovered, during a visit to her doctor on her return home, that she only needed to have the wax removed from her ears.

Realize that impairment of the inner ear can cause dizziness, a loss of equilibrium, and nausea. See your doctor if these symptoms appear.

Accidents

Among the elderly, accidents (falls, car mishaps, drownings, fire, and poison) frequently cause death and disability.

Why are we so susceptible to accidents as we age?

For one thing, we do not see as well as we used to. If we wear bifocals, we may find it difficult to appraise distances. We miss a step or trip over objects. Our night vision diminishes so that night driving becomes a risk. We may lose our balance, slip, or fall as a result of poor muscular coordination.

Since age reduces our ability to smell, we may not detect smoke or leaking gas.

Because 53 percent of all fatal accidents to persons over 65 occur in the home, we need to make use of every known home-safety device. Place guard rails on both sides of stairs. Install grab bars on bathtubs. Purchase nonskid carpets. Use a timer to alert you to food that is cooking or baking. Equip your home with smoke detectors.

Cirrhosis of the Liver

Certain infections, poisons, and a fatty or protein-impoverished diet actuate this degenerative disease in which the connective tissues thicken, then shrink, causing liver cells to waste away. The entire organ may become hard, yellow, lumpy, and shriveled.

As an irritant of the liver, alcohol induces a type of cirrhosis which affects people who drink excessively. Elderly persons who fail to cope with loneliness in the loss of spouse or friends, financial worries, or serious illnesses may turn to alcohol for escape. They are likely candidates for the disease.

*   *   *

Having read this chapter, you will have noticed how often proper diets, medication, exercise, and the avoidance of emotional stress and smoking underscore Dr. Sieglitz' affirmation that guarding and improving health—which is wealth—is as much a personal as it is a professional responsibility.

7

When Life Gets You Down

Stress, we have noted, frequently triggers hypertension, angina, and strokes. It can cause headaches and stomach upsets. Living with stress we become irritable, unhappy, and depressed.

Many people confuse anxiety with tension and stress. The terms do not have interchangeable meanings. Anxiety represents the uneasiness we feel when we anticipate real or imaginary threats. Tension and stress represent the frustration and at times despair we experience in attempting to cope with these threats. Do realize, however, that chronic anxiety evidenced by overanxious anticipation of imaginary or real threats often leads to stress.

Everyone reacts differently to experiences that may cause stress. You may consider a particular tense situation a challenge; another person may face it with fear. What appears an insurmountable problem to you may be a sowhat incident to a friend. A husband may chafe and fret when forced to be alone; his wife may welcome solitude.

How to Identify Stress

If an experience causes you to grit your teeth, tense your forehead, jaw, neck, and hand muscles or to complain of "butterflies" in the solar plexus, psychologists believe you ought to evaluate your reaction to the following questions:[1]

1. Do you worry a great deal of the time?
2. Are you usually edgy, irritable, and easily upset?
3. Do you fail to enjoy everyday pleasures?

75

4. Do you fear facing a new situation or meeting new people?
5. Are you suspicious and critical of others?
6. Is it difficult for you to get along with others?
7. Do you carry grudges?
8. Do you demean yourself, feel you are inferior or inadequate?
9. Do you wonder why you are so often moody and depressed?
10. Do you feel no one cares for you?

If you answer *yes* to only a few of these questions you may be experiencing only moderate tension. If most of the questions must be answered in the affirmative with an added "frequently" response, yours is more than ordinary tension.

Then what should you do?

Overcoming Tension

The National Association of Mental Health suggests:

* *Talk it out.* Don't bottle up your feelings. Confide in a sympathetic, understanding person in whose judgment and maturity you have confidence, a person whom you can trust to keep your problem confidential.

* *Escape from the problem for a time.* Remove yourself from the scene of conflict and frustration. A far-sighted view of the situation may clarify its significance and help you to evaluate it more sensibly. Don't sit and brood, however. Keep active.

* *Appraise the problem logically.* Tell yourself that this particular frustration is only temporary. You've experienced tension before, you'll experience it again. Realize, too, that stress isn't always bad. Under stress we often find ourselves. We need problems and challenges to help us find our gifts. Without stress we would stagnate spiritually and emotionally. To understand this is to live.

* *Get rid of your anger.* You won't be able to evaluate your problem if you flare up every time you think about it. Discarding anger may require articulating how you feel.

76

Further, try working out your anger. Wash the automobile, clean the refrigerator or stove. Mow the lawn. Go for a hike.

* *Learn to love yourself just as you are.* No one is perfect. All people don't possess the same intelligence, aptitudes, and skills. Everyone makes mistakes. You are no exception. Acknowledge this fact.

* *Be willing to mend broken fences.* If stress is caused by misunderstanding, even if you feel you are right, consider giving in once in awhile. An "I'm sorry" admission heals many a wound. It certainly brings peace of mind.

To the above list I would add:

* *Do not take more tranquilizers than your physician prescribes.* Overuse dulls your ability to appraise a situation properly.

* *Learn to relax.* Practice relaxing exercises. Meditate quietly in the presence of God. Take brief naps. I recall how often my mother cat-napped after lunch. When she'd come out of her bedroom shortly after entering it, I'd say, "Surely you haven't slept!"

Her answer: "Indeed I did. I feel fine now."

Stress Ratios

Sudden changes that occur in life patterns can produce stress in most people. In a 1967 study Dr. T. H. Holmes and Dr. R. H. Rahe rated the amount of stress resulting from interruptions and changes in 5,000 of their patients. Those which received the highest stress rating included: death of a spouse; marital separation; death of family members; personal injury or serious illness; loss of a job; retirement; change in financial status; loss of a friend.[2]

Note how many of the changes and interruptions of life patterns concern the elderly and that at the top of the list we find the loss of a spouse.

Though there are a great many more widows living today than there are widowers, the loss of a spouse creates a unique kind of stress for both groups of people. Being left alone means one must work one's way through grief and stress, with adjustment to the loss the ultimate goal.

We must learn to accept the loss as permanent. Not an easy thing to do. This takes time, agonizing time if a marriage was a loving, mutually happy one. The impulse to hurry home to share an experience with one's husband or wife does not disappear in a fortnight. Loneliness becomes a constant companion. If you find yourself in this situation you come to realize you are no longer a "couple" but a "third wheel" at social gatherings.

This type of stress also raises its ugly head when we lose close friends or experience illness. We may feel inclined to feel no one cares.

God made us resilient beings, however. We can work our way out of the stress that accompanies loneliness—*if* we recognize loneliness for what it is, a destroyer of happiness, an enemy that must not be pampered. One theologian says loneliness or the lonely preoccupation with self is a "poison to the mind."

When Nora Wenell lost her husband and two married sons within a three-year period of time, suffered a heart attack, and underwent cataract operations shortly afterward, family and friends were afraid she'd never be able to cope.

But she did. Like other widows she felt lonely, she grieved, but she didn't wallow in her grief. Today, at 83, she's one of the most well-adjusted widows I know. She works at a hospital-auxiliary thrift shop once a week. She's made piece quilts for all her grandchildren. She belongs to a crafts club and paints oil landscapes. Besides, she frequently invites friends in for evening or dinner fellowship. She attends church regularly. She never allowed a preoccupation with self to poison her mind.

In speaking of loneliness, we should realize that there is a vast difference between loneliness and aloneness. We need not be alone to be lonely. We can be lonely in a crowd. Being alone, occupied with an activity we enjoy, may be the balm needed to heal frustration and grief.

Personal injury and serious illness rank high on the list of changes and interruptions that cause great stress. My husband's stroke underscored this fact. Unexpected, it precipitated drastic change in his life-style.

He had planned to continue his interim work serving churches during intervals between regular pastors. The stroke, like a fierce gust of wind, slammed this door of service shut.

Although he is now much improved and anticipates complete recovery, there have been times of discouragement.

What caused the stroke?

Since my husband had just been given a clean bill of health following his annual medical checkup, we could not blame hypertension.

A vascular accident? Perhaps. If so, a series of circumstances that caused great anxiety precipitated my husband's illness. As we traveled to the Midwest from California, the automobile we had just purchased as a trustworthy, recently overhauled vehicle caused us a great deal of costly difficulty and delay—delay that meant the cancellation of important appointments.

Following the onslaught of the stroke we drove to the home of a sister, where we sought medical attention from a doctor friend. He suggested my husband rest and relax with my sister's family while I fulfilled an assignment at a Minneapolis writers' conference. If no change occurred in a week or nine days, we would be permitted to return to our home. At the end of that time we did return home.

At home we discussed the problem openly. My husband began a series of exercises to restore the mobility of his facial muscles. Each day he read aloud a chapter of a book we enjoyed, enunciating each syllable as distinctly as possible.

We constantly reminded each other that our frustration was only temporary. We'd experienced testing before; we might have to experience it again. We thanked God repeatedly that the stroke did not affect my husband's limbs. Too, when we looked at persons who endure much greater stress than we, we expressed gratefulness for our lot.

There are times when my husband's disgust flares anew when he thinks of the car which promised so much and delivered so little.

"Tut! Tut!" I say.

He understands. He knows he must rid himself of any animosity. We both realize he's making good progress in his stroke recovery. A two- or three-mile hike each day proves exhilarating. True, we've had to curtail certain social activities. And though my husband may never be able to pick up the work he loves, we remind ourselves that in quietness and peace God is our strength. Jesus said: "These things I have spoken unto you that in Me ye might have peace. In the world ye shall have tribulation; but be of good cheer, I have overcome the world" (John 16:33).

8

Forewarned/Forearmed

In dealing with concerns of the elderly, we find some of them do not fall into categories already discussed. Nevertheless, they deserve consideration.

Watch Your Overquotes

Take the matter of repetition, for instance. Many older persons tend to tell the same joke, the same story, or relate the details of a particularly meaningful experience over and over again. In doing so they alienate family and friends.

How can we avoid falling into this trap? Ask, "Have I told this before?" or enlist the help of family members in trying to overcome the "overquote habit." A woman who tried this scheme said: "At first I was embarrassed at how often I forgot, but correction made me use my mind and memory to overcome the repetition practice. Most families hesitate to correct a loved one, however, no matter how frequently he repeats himself. But if we indicate that we desire to be told, they will feel more free to offer correction."

In many instances older individuals neglect reading magazines, newspapers, and books. They don't put into their minds interesting knowledge they can retrieve when talking to others. Or they may not have developed hobbies, facts about which they can share. A word of caution here, however. "Shop" talk ordinarily interests only persons with similar concerns.

I can imagine myself listening eagerly to one of the "California Courtwatchers" describe the jury trial of a case in which I had special interest. I would enjoy hearing someone discuss a current best-seller I had not had time to read. I find a good Bible discussion stimulating if those who participate avoid parading biased opinions. I enjoy hearing someone discuss a particular passage of Scripture if he or she has done extensive research on the subject.

Be a Friend; Have a Friend

We've implied this before. As we age, our friends slip from us one by one. They move away from us or we move from them. Finding new friends isn't always easy. Yet it isn't as difficult as it first appears.

First, we need to strip ourselves of self-consciousness and/or fear of rejection. We do this when we realize there are many persons who occupy the same boat we do.

Since we make our most intimate friends in small-group gatherings, get involved in your local church. Join a senior-citizen choir or orchestra. Enroll in an adult education class that interests you. Do volunteer work. Write letters to family and friends from whom your move has separated you. Letters help you keep in contact; besides, they assure you of return mail. If you prefer, use postal cards to save time, effort, and money. A brief letter is better than none.

If you live in a retirement village make it a practice (if permissible) to sit with different residents at mealtime.

Travel Advice

In making travel plans, choose a trustworthy travel agency. Don't shun travel because you are unmarried, a widow, or a widower.

A woman accustomed to having her husband handle travel details profits most by joining a tour group where air fare, hotels, tips, and luggage handling are part of the package.

Some women enjoy pairing up with another female when making a trip. This isn't always advisable. Alone, a woman is not at the mercy of a companion's whims. She is free to pursue her own interests even if it means changing itinerary in mid-trip. Further, she may have an easier time making tour friends. Two women tend to hold themselves aloof from others. If you are wary of traveling alone, however, ask a friend to accompany you.

If you cannot afford to travel abroad, consider guided tours to nearby cities, national parks, or other points of interest. Ask your local church or senior-citizen organization for schedules of trips planned.

If you wear glasses, be sure you carry an extra pair or take your correction prescription with you.

1-209-632-3012

That's the telephone number my children have placed near their telephone along with police, fire department, and family doctor numbers—not just for emergency calls but for regular telephone visits with my husband and me.

A meaningful "Family Circus" cartoon explains why. The cartoon's first frame shows a white-haired grandmother standing by a window looking forlornly at trees shedding their fall leaves. The next frame depicts an ominous cloud, labeled LONELY, floating above her head. In the last picture her face lights up when the telephone jingles. A call from son, daughter, grandchildren? No doubt!

You don't need to wait for such a call, however. Jot down news you wish to share with your children and grandchildren. Jot down questions you wish to ask them. Then call them. Take advantage of night, early morning, and holiday discount rates. Whatever the rate, be aware that a visit by phone costs only a fraction of an automobile or airplane visit.

Car Worries

A director of a California retirement residence said he believes the most traumatic experience for an older person, next to losing his or her spouse, is to have to give up driving a car.

He may be right. While visiting a retirement complex in Florida one winter, my husband and I watched an elderly gentleman walk to a car in one of the parking lots. He crawled into the driver's seat and started the motor. But he didn't go anyplace. He sat with his hands on the steering wheel, play-acting for a half hour.

A daily ritual, the director told us. Why didn't he sell his car if he could no longer drive it? No way. It reminded him of experiences with which he could not bear to part.

Perhaps you have reached the point where you can no longer drive. This doesn't mean the world has come to an end. Most retirement residences provide transportation. If you live in your own home, dial-a-ride buses, city buses, and taxis are at your disposal. Taxi fare may be higher than that of buses, yet their occasional use cannot be compared to an automobile's gas, repair, depreciation, and replacement costs.

If you are one of the fortunate persons who have a great many driving years ahead of you, let caution be your creed. As we age, our reflexes slow down; we are not as alert as we used to be.

In moving to another state you will be required to obtain a driver's license no matter what the expiration date of your old one. In preparing for the new test, read your state's driving manual or vehicle code. Laws change from year to year and from state to state. Study road-sign shapes and meanings and speed limits in the area where you live.

Constantly remind yourself that a driver's license gives you the right to drive *protectively,* always alert to what other drivers might do.

"Golden" Wedding Bells

Much has been made of May-December marriages in recent years. Recall the interest evidenced when Ari Onassis, Pablo Casals, Leopold Stokowski, and Justice William Douglas took wives many years younger than they.

Marriages between persons over 65 don't make such headlines. Yet they represent an encouraging trend. In a study of 100 couples where the men were over 65 and the women over 60, sociologist Walter C. McKain of the University of Connecticut learned the husband and wife were friends of long standing or were related through marriage. Too, they were supported by friends who helped them face the disapproval of family and society. He also learned that good health, a zest for living and loving, and an ability to adjust to change made good marriages.

I believe many of the principles that make a good marriage in youth apply to people who marry after retirement: mutual interests, a common faith, adequate finances, a reputable character.

The latter requirement cannot be ignored. If you contemplate a "late" marriage, don't hesitate to investigate your prospective mate's finances and his or her reputation. I am personally acquainted with two widows who had their marriages annulled shortly after the wedding took place. I surmise they failed to investigate the character, finances—whatever—of the men they wed. Or the men cunningly fooled them.

No-Cost Gifts

Birthdays, anniversaries, Christmas, these are gift-giving events which, because of limited funds, you may have come to dread.

You need not fear them. Realize that "the gift without the giver is bare." Give yourself. Prepare a gift certificate which indicates the talent, skill, or time you wish to present to a neighbor, a friend, a grandchild, or a nursing-home resident. Come birthday, Christmas, or anniversary, place the certificate in a small box and gift-wrap it for delivery with love.

Some suggestions:

* To a grandson: I will play Racko, Scrabble, or
                     Monopoly with you once a week.

* To a daughter:	I will bake bread when you entertain for special occasions.
* To a son:	This certificate is good for 10 baby-sitting sessions.
* Neighbor:	I will take you to your doctor for your monthly cancer (whatever) treatment.
* Granddaughter:	10 knitting, art, crotcheting (whatever) lessons.

That's a start. Now you complete the list.

A potpourri of suggestions. May they enrich your life as you grow old.

9

If Senility Strikes
Your Loved One

I shall never forget the day a sister who was caring for our aged mother wrote, "Mom built a fire in the kitchen wastebasket today. Her explanation: 'It's raining outside.'"

Later, "Her doctor attributes her senility to cerebral arteriosclerosis. She must be watched constantly. I can't care for her much longer. I'm exhausted. Would you take her for awhile?"

"I can try," I answered, gratefully aware of how much this sister and her husband had sacrificed when they sold their home some thousand miles away and moved in with Mother. I understood, too, how weary they must be.

I assumed Mother's care shortly afterward. I'd be lying if I said it was easy. Some experiences were amusing—as the time she took food from our daughter's plate and gave it to my husband, who had already eaten his. Other experiences were heartbreaking—Mother visiting with a magazine picture of our President as if he were a guest in our home. I blinked tears frequently as I recalled the intelligent, perceptive mother of my youth.

I can't say I ever became angry with her. I loved her, but I also pitied her. Some senile persons change personalities as their illness progresses. They become belligerent, demanding a second meal after the first one. They may even accuse someone in the family of mistreating them. Mother never did. She remained the kind, patient person she'd always been. Nevertheless we had to watch her constantly lest she stray from the house, burn herself, or lose her way to the bathroom.

Like my sister, I grew weary as I cared for her. After some months the constant supervision by day and broken sleep at night caused the flare-up of a previous back ailment. One night in my haste to help Mother find the bathroom I ruptured a disk in my back so badly that surgery became necessary.

Mother was moved to the home of another sister, where three small children complicated her care. It was then our family began to investigate alternate care facilities. Nursing homes proved too costly—no medicare then! Mother's doctor recommended a state hospital. Unthinkable, we siblings countered.

"If your mother broke her hip or suffered incurable cancer, you would place her where she would be cared for properly, wouldn't you?" my surgeon asked. "Mental illness shouldn't be thought of differently. And remember, in this state no one is committed to any of our state hospitals without court consent and the recommendation of two physicians who agree such care is mandatory."

Reluctantly I signed the legal document that required family consent for such placement.

When I had sufficiently recovered from surgery, I visited Mother frequently. One day I spoke to the psychiatrist who cared for her. "Isn't there any cure?" I asked.

"Unfortunately not," the man answered. "No known therapy is effective in this illness. Different medications are intermittently in vogue, but we have found none that is satisfactory. Tranquilizers help persons most disturbed.

"Any future successful treatment must lie in prevention therapy. There are doctors who believe a low cholesterol diet helps. My hope is that medical research will come up with something that offers more promise than the medications which are available now."

Unknown to me and no doubt to him, this man's hope was being fulfilled even as he spoke. Today doctors affirm reversal and cure as well as prevention, depending on the cause of senility.

Be aware that when they speak of senescence (the state of being or growing old) in reference to persons 65 or over, they do not imply mental deterioration or any particular emotional problem. When they describe an elderly individual as being senile, they mean this person displays specific symptoms of confusion, disorientation, and memory loss.

We need to realize, however, that these symptoms arise from various types of brain disorders, which may be acute or chronic in nature. Acute brain disorders, which usually appear suddenly, are temporary and often reversible. Their cause: infections, congestive heart failure, too much medication, uremia, liver diseases, alcoholism, and vitamin deficiencies.

Disturbances of memory, orientation, and intellectual functioning fluctuate. Fear and apprehension are common; hallucinations and illusions may be present.

The chronic brain disorders do not surface as quickly, though memory impairment, changes in intellectual functions, and emotional instability may result. The two most common causes of chronic brain disorders are brain diseases (deterioration of the brain cells, brain tumors, enlarged cerebral ventricles) and arteriosclerosis (hardening of the cerebral arteries).

In her 50s Anne became extremely nervous and depressed. Her doctor surmised menopause difficulties. Gradually her condition worsened, however. She grew forgetful. Confused, she often mistook one member of the family for another. Today she may cut her bread with a spoon, eat soup with a knife, or disrobe completely several times a day. The diagnosis: senility caused by deterioration of the brain cells, for which no known cause or cure has been found.

A few years ago, Lon, a clergyman, began having excruciating headaches. After undergoing extensive tests the doctors discovered a brain tumor at the base of his skull. Its removal also involved the removal of the pituitary gland. He was given medication to compensate for its loss.

Several years passed without incidence. He moved to a new, promising parish. Then suddenly the headaches recurred. He found it difficult, often impossible to study. When he preached, he forgot whole segments of his sermon. He often said things that embarrassed his wife. "I'm afraid Lon's becoming senile," his wife wrote his kin.

Specialists discovered a new brain tumor. Recovery? Unpredictable.

A team of surgeons headed by Henry A. Shenkin[1] discovered that Sarah, one of several patients at the Episcopal Hospital in Philadelphia, suffered from senility caused by hydrocephalus, a condition marked by excessive fluid and pressure in the cranial cavity. In some instances the disease causes atrophy of the brain.

In making their diagnosis of the disease, the doctors removed the fluid from the cavity, replacing it with air. The amount of air that filled the cavity revealed whether or not the ventricles were enlarged. In Sarah's case they were. Treatment: Sarah underwent a ventricular shunt. Surgeons inserted a tube into the brain, ran it down the neck under the skin and through the body into the abdominal cavity, where it drains the excessive fluid.

Sarah is one of 18 out of 28 patients in one test who lost their senility with this treatment.

Though advanced senility caused by cerebral arteriosclerosis may not be reversible, many patients in the early stages of the disease can be helped by the replacement or reaming of arteries that feed the brain.

Fred, a Nebraska farmer in his late 80s, grew increasingly forgetful. Problems he ordinarily solved without difficulty proved incomprehensible. In examining him, an Omaha specialist discovered sludging and blockage in the arteries on the sides of his neck leading to the brain.

The doctor performed an operation called an endarterectomy, which cleaned the main artery, first on one side of Fred's neck and head, then on the other. Symptoms of senility disappeared. He lived well into his 90s without further mental disability.

Dr. James C. Folsom and Dr. Geneva S. Folsom describe an 82-year-old man whose senile responses were triggered and accentuated by isolation and shock.[2]

While on his way to visit his two sons, he failed to stop for a red light. He was hit by a truck. Unconscious, he was taken to a hospital, where a pin was placed in his hip.

When he regained consciousness, no one bothered to tell him his name. A nurse entered the room, rolled him over, and gave him a sedative without revealing her identity. Her only information: "You were in a wreck."

There were no calendars on the wall, no clock to tell time. When the man's sons came to see what had happened to him, he recognized them but wasn't sure which of his seven they were. When his wife, whom he had recently married, arrived, the man called her by his first wife's name. She didn't bother to correct him.

By the time two noninformative days had passed, he was genuinely confused.

He awakened one night to find someone standing over him with a pillow. He thought this person was trying to smother him. He struggled to escape and had to be subdued.

His sons were called and told, "Your father is irrational. We have had to tie him down and sedate him heavily." Because of his age, *senile* was recorded on his chart. No one expected him to recover.

But he did recover. According to the two Dr. Folsoms, someone trained in the use of reality orientation (RO) intervened and instructed the family and hospital staff how to communicate with him. Doctors and nurses were told to call him by name every time they entered the room.

The family members were told to say, "Dad, I'm Jeff" — and to remind their father of the time of the day and the day of the week.

His wife brought him the daily newspaper. She showed him the dateline and the weather report. She read the current events to him. She also prepared him for the next meal. "In an hour you will have dinner," she'd tell him.

Hospital personnel told him exactly what medication he was being given, why and how it would be administered.

In a very short time the confusion lifted and the undeserved "senile" diagnosis was dropped.

In researching reality orientation further, I found that the idea for this treatment of senile patients originated at the Menninger Foundation, Topeka, Kans. Its files contain a great many case histories of institutionalized persons who were able to return to their homes and manage for themselves after receiving this type of personalized care.

Reality orientation has been tested extensively by the Geriatric Treatment Service of the Veterans Administration Hospital, Tuscaloosa, Ala., under the direction of Dr. James C. Folsom and Dr. L. R. Taulbee. It has also been endorsed by the American Medical Association's Committee on Aging.

A section in the book *Current Psychiatric Therapies, Volume 7,* also affirms this type of treatment.[3] I recap its basic principles:

First, the patient is led to reaffirm his identity. Then he is given other basic information about his current life situation—his home address, his telephone number, and other related information.

Occasionally a patient believes certain relatives, long since dead or removed from the home, are still present. He is helped to comprehend the fact that they are gone. No attempt is made to protect him from the truth.

Treatment, 24-hour-a-day intensive reality orientation therapy, encompasses every activity in which the patient is involved. At meals someone identifies items of food and talks about them. A patient may need to be told, "This is your spoon, Mr. James. Pick it up and eat your cereal with it."

92

In its initial phases this type of care and concern becomes exceedingly time-consuming. But when doctors, hospital or nursing-home staff, and family work as a team utilizing these procedures, recovery results surprise everyone.

Pondering this procedure, my thoughts go to several senile persons I have known. I think of a charming elderly woman, Susana Clemens, 72, whom I visited in her room on the nursing-home floor reserved for senile patients.

I found her bustling around her room. "Packing for a trip," she told me. I watched as she gathered bits of cloth, several handkerchiefs, and a few pieces of jewelry and packed them in a small traveling case her family had given her.

She said good-bye to me, left the room, and began her trek down the corridor and back. Entering the room, she greeted me joyously. As she unpacked she described her trip in detail, no doubt recalling one she had taken as a child.

By the time I was ready to leave she had begun to pack again. Packing and unpacking—these activities filled her lonely day.

In retrospect I catch myself wondering if she or Mother could have been helped by reality orientation. Doctors whom I have consulted negate such a possibility since Susana and Mother suffered from advanced cerebral arteriosclerosis.

In the March 31, 1973 issue of the *National Observer* an article gives direction for handling a situation where we suspect a loved one of becoming senile. Quoting Dr. J. C. Folsom, it admonishes us to avoid endorsing senile behavior. "We reward the aged for being forgetful," he says. "We say, 'Oh, mother has lost her glasses. Let's help look.' Then mother realizes that's the only way she can get attention."

Additional advice: Give older persons magnifying glasses to help them read. Encourage them to do everything they can for themselves. Listen to them, share ideas, empathize with their concerns. Reinforce their identity and self-esteem.

The doctor who supervised my mother's care said it didn't matter whether she recognized us or not. Our very presence during visits caused her to sense that someone cared and was concerned about her. So don't neglect showing love to the person who has become senile.

I would also add: Study reality orientation procedures. Put them into practice. Encourage local hospital and nursing homes to try this method of reversing senile symptoms.

What can we do to avoid becoming senile? Not much, if heredity can be pinpointed as the cause. On the other hand, doctors advise fostering intellectual pursuits—and avoiding foods which may cause cerebral arteriosclerosis.

10

Health Care:
Home vs. Institutional

If anyone asked you what you want more than anything as you grow old, chances are you would say that you wish to be able to care for yourself as long as you possibly can. Most people cherish the same desire, and rightly so.

According to a U. S. government survey, approximately 25 percent of all older patients in hospitals and nursing homes need not be there. But because these people are unable to prepare meals or manage household chores or because they need some type of weekly therapy, they are institutionalized at great cost to the taxpayers and at great psychological expense to themselves.[1]

If your spouse is living, count yourself fortunate. You may be able to care for each other during a bout of illness or following a period of hospitalization. If you live alone, you may consider hiring someone to take care of you in your home.

There are instances when home care of husband, wife, or parents presents innumerable problems, however. This is especially true when the recipient of the care displays senile behavior. Nevertheless many persons find such service rewarding. A cousin who cared for her husband, a retired Los Angeles businessman, for several years following his heart attack and mental disorientation chose not to place him in a nursing home.

"Home care has advantages even in such circumstances," she says. "I was able to supervise Harry's diet as well as to monitor his medication. Cost proved minimal compared to the $650 a month paid by a friend over a period of years for nursing home care for her husband.

"When I drove through the streets of Los Angeles, he served as my male protector. No one suspected he was incapable of taking care of me!

"He enjoyed church and the singing of hymns that were familiar to him. I recall the day our congregation sang, 'When Christ shall come, with shouts of acclamation . . . ' He nudged me, and his face lit up like the Fourth of July.

"Disadvantages?

"I was terribly tied down. I rarely had a moment to myself. When I shopped, wherever I went, I had to watch my husband constantly lest he stray. Yet in spite of my diligence he managed to lose himself a couple of times. One night he walked for miles before he was found. I'll admit there were times when I despaired. Yet, were you to ask me if I would do it again, I'd answer emphatically, 'Indeed I would!' "

There are many people who feel as this woman does. Aroused, they have prompted Congress to examine ways of expanding home-health services. As a result, the Nurses Training and Revenue Sharing Act, passed in 1975, provides funds for the development of new health agencies and for staff training.

Unquestionably home-health care is cheaper than hospital and nursing home care. The April/May 1976 issue of *Modern Maturity* contains an article which emphasizes this point.[2] In a particular instance the cost of home care (which included 29 visits from a registered nurse, 16 from a physical therapist, 96 from home-health aides, and 3 from a social worker) following hospitalization resulting from an automobile accident came to $3,500, or $25 per day, for 141 days. Without home care the patient mentioned would have been hospitalized for 74 days at a cost of $8,500.

Medicare pays home-care benefits under both *hospital insurance (Part A)* and *medical insurance (Part B)*.

You qualify under *Medicare hospital insurance* if you meet the following conditions:

1. You were in a qualified hospital for at least three days in a row.
2. Home-health care is for further treatment of the condition for which you were hospitalized or for which you were treated in a skilled nursing facility.
3. The care you need includes part-time skilled nursing care, physical or speech therapy.
4. You are confined to your home.
5. A doctor has determined you need home-health care and has set up a plan for your care within 14 days of your discharge from a hospital.
6. The home-health agency that provides the care is a participant in Medicare.

If you qualify under these stipulations, hospital insurance pays the full cost up to 100 visits during a benefit period.

Medicare medical insurance pays for 100 home-health visits in a year without hospital admission if:

1. You need part-time skilled nursing care, physical or speech therapy.
2. A doctor recommends such services and sets up a home-care program for you.
3. You are confined to your home.
4. The home-health agency is a participant in Medicare.

After you have met the yearly deductible, Medicare pays full costs for home visits. The home-health agency you use submits claims in your behalf.

Because regulations and costs change frequently, anyone who wishes to take advantage of Medicare benefits should consult local offices for updated information.

For persons unable to prepare their own meals, the nationwide Meals-on-Wheels program offers nutritional food at a minimal price. Lloyd, a retired salesman, wishes to care for his wife, who suffers from a muscle-deteriorating disease, in their mobile home as long as he

97

can. When she could no longer do the cooking, he appealed to the local Meals-on-Wheels volunteers. Now two hot, nutritious meals are delivered to their home each noon.

When Nursing Home Care is Recommended

Most experts agree that as long as an older person is able to cope mentally and physically with life outside of an institution he or she should be encouraged to do so. Nevertheless, no matter how much home-health care is applauded, it is not recommended for families who are unable to care for family members between professional visits. Bedridden patients without families, as well as fearful, lonely persons may feel more comfortable and secure in a rest home or a skilled nursing facility.

These two facilities differ in that a rest home merely provides custodial care—the type you would expect to receive in your own home if someone were able and willing to assume it: help with grooming, bathing, dressing; assistance from bed to wheelchair; meals; and in some instances supervised recreation.

Skilled nursing homes provide around-the-clock nursing services and medical supervision as an extension of hospital care. Registered nurses, licensed practical nurses, and aides serve you as recommended by your physician. A good home not only provides nursing care but rehabilitation services, physical and occupational therapy. If a person qualifies, Medicare and Medicaid programs pay for skilled nursing-home care. You may pick up information about these programs, and percentage of costs covered, at your local Social Security office.

Be aware, however, that nursing homes are not required to participate in these financial aid programs. In such instances patients foot their own nursing-home expenses.

Our Social Security program finances nursing-home costs covered by Medicare if the following conditions are met:

1. The home is a skilled-nursing facility.

2. The patient has spent at least three consecutive days in a hospital and admittance to the nursing home occurs within 14 days after discharge from the hospital.
3. The doctor certifies that extended care is needed for the same related illness for which the person was hospitalized.
4. The patient requires continuous skilled nursing or daily rehabilitation services.

Does the thought that someday, because of your health, you may be required to accept nursing-home care appall you? It may if you recall all the magazine and newspaper stories you have read which expose nursing homes as institutions with untrained staffs, dilapidated buildings, inadequate medical and personal care, as well as unscrupulous operators.

These types of homes do exist. In too large numbers, it seems. In his book *Growing Old in the Country of the Young,* Charles H. Percy attacks and exposes these facilities for what they are.[3] Then he contrasts them with a home he describes as "ideal"—a nonprofit Illinois home affiliated with the United Church of Christ. There residents are treated with respect and with a genuine concern for their personal needs.

This particular facility provides both "community" and residential care. It delivers two meals (one a hot lunch) five days a week to elderly men and women in its vicinity who are unable to cook for themselves. Its day-care center offers physical and occupational therapy or just a place where the elderly can come and visit during the day.

Residents, Percy recounts, are treated as members of a family. Upon entrance they choose their own room, in some instances selecting the color they would like to have it painted.

Skilled medical personnel strive to rehabilitate and to minimize discomfort. Nutritious meals are served appealingly. Activities include Bible study, crafts, and sewing. A beauty and barber shop keep residents well groomed.

The home owns a 12-passenger station wagon which takes residents shopping, to the library, to church, on picnics, and to nearby athletic events.

Of greatest importance, perhaps, is that the facility operates on a 1-to-3 ratio of staff members and residents. Medical and nursing staff, aides and volunteers receive periodic in-service training so they can respond more compassionately to the needs of the residents.

This home represents many which dispense tender, loving personal care—fun, too. Recently several elderly women nursing-home residents participated in a local "My Fair Lady" contest sponsored by the County Fair. The winner, an 82-year-old wheelchair resident of a church-affiliated home, captured the "My Fair Lady" title as much by her witty, perceptive answers to the judges' questions as by her charm.

Speaking of nursing home care a doctor once said: "I believe nonprofit, church-related nursing homes dispense more tender, loving care than do those which operate for a profit."

So, when and if a nursing home becomes the only option for extended care for a loved one, do some preliminary shopping before you make your choice. Visit the facility several times. Talk to residents. Check cleanliness, food, and personal concern.

Better yet, become acquainted with nursing homes in your area before you need this type of care.

11

On Death and Dying

The fact we are growing old presupposes some knowledge of death and dying. We've known what it means to lose friends and loved ones. Nevertheless, we don't feel comfortable when we contemplate the imminence of our own death. No doubt you, as I, have wondered how you would cope were you told you had only a short time to live. A very meaningful short story dramatizes the reaction of a clergyman who faced this problem.[1]

Driving to his home following a consultation with his doctor, the clergyman pondered what he should tell his wife and teenage son. Regretfully, he wished he had at least one act of heroism and daring to leave them. He could think of none.

After he had parked his car a careful six inches from the curb in front of his home, he sat for a moment praying for self-control. Then he slipped from the car, squared his shoulders, and, forcing a jaunty whistle from his lips, strode toward the house.

He found his son sitting beside the living room window, a newspaper limp in his hands. The boy's bewildered, frightened eyes revealed that somehow he had learned the truth.

"You know?" the father stammered. "How?"

"A man from the clinic called. He thought he was talking to you. He wanted to know the name of our family doctor."

The father told him he was sorry. Then, "I wanted to tell . . ."

Weeping the boy threw himself into his father's arms. When he raised his head and wiped his tears, he looked at his father through shiny eyes of awe.

"You're really something, Dad. I watched you as you drove up. You're braver than anyone I know. You whistled . . . !"

We can look at this story as a parable. As such it implies the lead character did have an act of heroism to leave his son. Courageous in spite of his fear and distress, he built sustaining rapport with the boy. Knowing he had planned to share his problem with both his wife and his son, we can surmise that together they faced the inevitable with fortitude and love. Which is as it should be. The historian Arnold Toynbee once said: "The negation of life's fulfillment is synonymous with the refusal to accept its ending."[2] To live fully, he implies, indicates a willingness to deal openly with the inevitable—death.

Death was no stranger to our forefathers. When it resulted from infectious diseases, it struck down persons of all ages. And when older persons passed away, often in the same house or in a house nearby, the children and grandchildren were a part of the scene.

This was true of Biblical characters, too. Recall how the patriarchs called their children to their bedside when death appeared imminent. In such a setting they reaffirmed their faith in God, discussed the future with their children, and blessed them.

You and I may never have that option, however. Today, shunted off to nursing homes and hospitals, the terminally ill are isolated from their loved ones. Too often the truth concerning their illness and imminent death is withheld from them.

When I consider these facts a host of questions push their way into my mind. Let's look at them together.

Should the Terminally Ill Be Told They Will Die?

Suppose a married man, the father of several children,

undergoes a cancer operation from which there is no hope of recovery. No one tells him the seriousness of his illness. When he insists on knowing when he will be able to return home, he is told he first must have a few more tests or that he must gain more strength.

Too late he realizes the doctors and members of his family have not been honest with him. Had they discussed his problem openly, he could have planned the future with his wife. He could have made necessary decisions concerning his business affairs. He might even have planned his funeral.

Understanding she had only a few months to live, unless God performed a miracle, the mother of some teenage girls spent a great deal of time preparing them for life without her. Together they discussed the problems of sex, dating, education, careers, and marriage. She taught them details about housekeeping, sewing, and cooking. More important, she demonstrated a trust and faith in God they'll never be able to forget.

Though most doctors believe the terminally ill have the right to know the truth, there are those who qualify this right by insisting the attending physician supply only as much information as the patient desires and asks for. If a patient says, "I don't want to know," the doctor should respect that wish. Invariably, the patient reverses this decision, however, and asks to be told the truth.

Most physicians insist that under no circumstances should death dates be set, however. "Only God knows when a person will die," a doctor friend told me recently. "I've sent patients home to die who I felt had but a few months to live, only to have them come bouncing into my office a couple of years later, seemingly in the best of health.

"In one instance I gave up completely on a patient. He had every complication in the book. Yet three months later he walked out of the hospital fully recovered."

Many times members of the immediate family will object to a patient's being told he has a terminal illness.

They insist, "He or she can't handle the truth," when in reality it is they who are unable to cope.

It's very likely, however, that the patient already knows. The physician is elusive; he no longer lingers to chat. Nurses delay responding to his light and hurry off when they do. Members of the family are uneasy in his presence.

How Should We Treat a Loved One Who Is Dying?

Specialists in the field are extremely concerned about our attitudes toward the dying. At the very time they need us most, we shun them.

A Christian doctor claims that at no other time is it as necessary to demonstrate the "fruits of the Spirit": love, joy, peace, patience, gentleness, goodness, and faith.

We must be willing to listen. A loved one may need to unburden a guilt, a fear, or ask some favor. We should visit the dying frequently, particularly when the end is near. Our presence will comfort and reassure. Above all else we should demonstrate our love, touch, embrace, whatever.

I recall the day I visited a man I'll call John, who had been paralyzed from his neck down in a construction accident. Because he had been extremely ill, the hospital barber had been unable to cut his hair. Anticipating out-of-town visitors, John's wife, who knew I had cut my son's hair when he was young, asked me if I would cut her husband's hair.

When I finished, I ran my hand through John's hair. "I wish there was something else I could do for you."

Quickly he answered, "You can rub my head."

Just a touch, but extremely meaningful to one shut away from the world.

Further, we need to understand the stages through which a dying person goes when he faces death.

What Are the Stages
Through Which Dying Persons Pass?

From hundreds of interviews, Dr. Elisabeth Kubler-

Ross[3] learned that dying persons pass through five emotional stages in varying lengths of time before they die. The first is shock, which manifests itself in *denial.* Patients shake their heads and say, "Not me. It can't be me." Denial, Dr. Kubler-Ross says, is customarily as true of patients who are told the truth about their condition outright as it is of those who come to this conclusion by themselves.

The second stage is *anger.* When the denial cannot be sustained any longer, anger, rage, envy, and bitterness surface. "Why me?" a patient asks, "why not her?" "Why should she be allowed to enjoy her grandchildren?" "It isn't fair! I don't want to die!"

In this stage the patient may take out his spite and rage on everyone and everything. Of all stages this may be the most difficult for the family to cope with unless they empathetically place themselves in the patient's situation and imagine how they would feel.

In the third phase the dying person goes through a period of *bargaining.* "God, I'll attend church every Sunday, if You . . .." "If I live, I'll do anything You want me to do." Or the patient may want to live for an important event: a grandchild's birth, until a man's son returns from a business assignment abroad. Strangely, the bargaining never ceases. As one deadline is met another is proposed.

Eventually the patient goes into a fourth stage, *depression.* The burden becomes too great. To have to leave everything, family, friends, independence . . . The ill person may withdraw and become uncommunicative. Those who stand by should not minimize this depression but support the one who grieves. This support may come through the Scriptures, the quiet reading of Psalm 23 or similar comforting passages.

This step leads to stage five, acceptance, the time when the patient says, "Soon I will die." It is at this stage, more than any other, that the terminally ill may express concern about a hereafter. Previously in forced gaity or grumbling they have attempted to cover up the fear or anxiety they feel.

Over a period of many months I corresponded and talked over long-distance telephone with a friend who I knew suffered a terminal illness. Her joshing, blasé attitude grieved me. I could not move beyond it.

Then without any previous warning she asked if she could visit me.

I recall those days with joy. The defenses were down. Together we openly discussed what it means to have the assurance of eternal life with God. I realize that I would not have had that privilege had I not "stood by" during the denial stage of her illness.

As you watch a loved one go through each stage, be aware that you may experience similar emotions. You may be angry at God for allowing the illness to occur, at doctors for not effectively halting the disease. You too may bargain: just a little more time together.

What Happens When a Person Dies?

Until recently the final heartbeat and the last breath marked the end of life. Today, because of medical advances, which include portable respirators, external heart massage, electronic pacemakers, new drugs, heart-lung machines, improved heart surgery, both the heart and the lungs can often be resuscitated after they have stopped. Thus doctors are moving away from the traditional focus on respiration and heartbeat to the consideration of "brain death," which means the cells have been denied oxygen to the extent that they die. When this happens, the brain-wave recordings do not appear wavy as they normally would, but flatten to indicate the brain cells have died.

A patient is pronounced dead when he is totally unaware and unresponsive, so that even the most painful stimuli fail to evoke a vocal or physical response. Reflexes are absent. The pupils of his eyes are dilated and unresponsive to bright light. The soul has departed; its earthly home remains.

When doctors broadened the definition of death to include the absence of brain activity, they anticipated easier access to human organs for transplants. Under new laws in several states, doctors must keep the heart and lungs going while the brain is tested. Once the brain is dead, it is assumed the donor's organs may be removed safely.

How Does One Go About Leaving Part of One's Body to Science?

Thirty-nine states have passed laws that simplify the donating of one's body to science. Anyone can donate an organ or the entire body by putting this request in his will, or "by any written document," including a small card that can be carried in a wallet. If you wish to use the donor card, you only need to sign it and have it signed by two witnesses. Cards and explanatory material can be obtained from a number of sources. (See appendix.)

Should Doctors Prolong Life Through Artificial Means?

This is perhaps the most agonizingly debatable question facing the medical profession. A magazine article presents several case histories which illustrate the problem.[4] I refer you to two of them.

An elderly patient with inoperable cancer has a heart attack. Prompt treatment with strong drugs coupled with the use of advanced coronary-care equipment may prevent immediate death. But if the patient pulls through, all he can look forward to is additional pain and eventual death from cancer. Should the intensive care be withheld?

In another instance a 33-year-old man was brought into the emergency room of a New York hospital following an overdose of heroin. He was not breathing. Tests revealed his brain had been permanently damaged. If he lived he would always be a human vegetable. Should the lung

107

pump be used to revive the patient or should he be declared dead?

These are not easy questions. Doctors are trained to sustain life, yet there is growing concern about whether the life of a terminally ill patient should be extended at excessive costs and in many instances prolonged suffering.

The only advice I can offer is that you consult your doctor and clergyman when the extension of life affects a loved one. If it involves your own life, you have the option to confer with them now, and to indicate your wishes regarding the extension of your own life through artificial means.

How Can We Cope with Grief?

Without doubt no loss is as great for older persons as that of a spouse whom one has loved and with whom one has shared the greatest portion of one's life.

A widower who recently lost his wife said, "I feel like half a person."

Grieving in these instances is normal; not to grieve is abnormal. It is true those of us who are Christians "sorrow not as those who have no hope," but we do sorrow.

Immediately following a funeral the grief-stricken survivor may experience restlessness and engage busily in activities that were meaningful to the deceased.

Or he may experience a period of denial when he refuses to accept the death as final. The grieving person may keep a workroom intact or refuse to dispose of clothing and other reminders of the deceased.

No one ever fully recovers from the loss of a loved one. Eventually, however, the wound heals and only a faint scar remains to indicate its reality.

We who stand by are meant to help the sorrowing person work through his grief. We can do this best by reminiscing about the good times we have enjoyed with the deceased and by allowing the survivor to talk freely about their life together, from the time they met, were married, had children, took trips, whatever.

Too often we shower food, love, and attention on the sorrowing at the time of death and forget to sustain these people through the weeks and months when the finality of death becomes increasingly traumatic.

You may find that a grieving friend expresses anger at the loved one for leaving the other to cope alone. Or he is angry with God for allowing death to take place. This, too, is natural. A bachelor until middle life, C. S. Lewis found fulfillment and happiness in a brief marriage to a woman who died of cancer a few years after he married her.

He speaks of his grief in *A Grief Observed.*[5] "O God, God," he wrote, "why did you take such trouble to force this creature out of its shell if it is now doomed to crawl back—to be sucked back—into it?"

I emphathized fully with Joseph Bayly when I read his poem, "A Psalm on the Death of My 18-Year-Old Son."[6] In the poem he calls God, "Spoiler of my treasure."

Yet I am reassured to realize he was working out his grief when he ended the poem, "Have mercy, God, here is my quitclaim."

You may also find that a grieving person experiences guilt following a loved one's death. "If only I had gone to another doctor . . ." Or, "I could have been kinder and more sympathetic." This too will pass. We all make mistakes. I still feel regret that I was unable to care for my senile mother during the last months of her life. Yet I know God understands.

In coping with death we need to understand that death is a nasty wound and that it takes time for the wound to heal. But we must, by an effort of will, want it to heal. If we pick at the scab, healing is delayed.

What About Funerals?

Much has been written in recent years about unscrupulous funeral directors who are out to make a large profit out of every funeral.

My husband and I have known many morticians during our lifetime. For the most part they have been understanding and kind. In fact one of our friends had to give up his work because his wife was too kind. She entered into the sorrow of each funeral as if it were hers.

We do know, however, that in some instances funerals—caskets, burial plots, mortician fees—are overpriced. The point is, we have the option to make whatever arrangements we choose unless the deceased has previously made them.

Included in the basic fee are costs involved in the removal of the corpse to the funeral home, preparation of the body for burial, and the use of funeral home facilities and personnel.

When you consult the funeral director about arrangements, you will indicate when you prefer the funeral to be held. Often this is determined by the time it takes distant relatives and friends to arrive. You will indicate a burial or cremation preference. Today many large cities encourage cremation, a procedure which may be a faster, cleaner way for the body to return to dust—less costly, too.

You will indicate whether you wish to use the funeral-home chapel or your local church for the service. Many pastors prefer that funerals of church members be held in church, where other significant events in the deceased person's life have been observed.

You will express your desires regarding the viewing of the body. Personally I dislike the viewing of a body at the funeral service. Were I to agree to a viewing, it would be held at the funeral home the evening before the funeral, with a private committal service with the immediate family later that evening or the next morning.

Then a memorial service without the casket present would be held to honor the one who had passed away.

Though I prefer eliminating the viewing service entirely, I realize there are people with whom death-denial is a problem. For such people an open casket and a viewing serve to comfort and to heal.

Do realize that you can make any decisions, including choice of speakers, music, and type of service, you prefer. Don't let other people influence you to do something you don't wish to do.

Increasingly the memorial service is planned to be an affirmation of the resurrection of the Lord Jesus Christ, as well as the resurrection of our loved one who believed in Him. Shortly before Dwight L. Moody died, he verbalized this affirmation. "Soon you will read in the newspapers that Moody is dead," he said. "Don't you believe it, for I shall be more alive then than I am now."

12

Faith in Your Future

In my association with people who are growing old, I find many persons who have known and loved God the Father and His Son Jesus Christ from their youth. They anticipate a hereafter we call heaven.

Others once knew God, but they turned their backs and walked away from Him. They are like the prodigal son, the waster in Jesus' parable, who sought a life apart from his father. Recently the implications of this parable struck me with new significance. I realized for the first time that, when the son repents and returns to his father, no mention is made of his age. He could have been an old man! It didn't matter. The father rushed to meet him and to welcome him back with joy.

If you identify with the prodigal, realize that you, too, can come back to God. You, too, can reaffirm your faith in Him.

When I researched the life of the infamous turn-of-the-century Minnesota outlaw John Whitman Sornberger, alias Jack McWilliams, a few years ago, I discovered how much he resembled the prodigal son.

Though reared in a Christian home, he turned his back on God. At 16 he apprenticed to the rugged life of a woodsman. One day he was introduced to professional boxing. For eight years he held the championship in two divisions of the ring.

Success went to his head. He turned to booze and women, lost his money and his fame. For lack of funds for liquor he robbed saloons and "blind-pig" establishments. Before long he was shooting it out with bootleggers and lawmen.

Eventually he was wanted in four states, and sheriffs in every county in Minnesota were searching for him.

He found refuge in an isolated northwoods logging camp. One day Frank Higgins, itinerant lumberjack missionary, visited the camp. After dinner he pulled out his Bible and began to preach . . . about the prodigal's father!

When Higgins described the prodigal's home, he sent the lumberjacks back over memory's lane into their own childhood homes. There they enjoyed the cozy warmth of the old homestead barrel stove. They devoured huge plates of Mother's savory food, basked in Father's prudent care.

Then Higgins zeroed in on the prodigal's adventures, so like those of the men to whom he was speaking. He told of the prodigal's downfall and his repentance, then of his joyous return to a forgiving father. He likened the father to God.

Banging his fist on a table, Sornberger rose. Cursing bitterly, he strode from the room. Frank Higgins sought him out.

"No way would God take *me* back," Sornberger told the man. But God did take him back. He forgave all his crimes, as did the Honorable John Johnson, Christian governor of Minnesota, who pardoned him and welcomed him back into the family of God.

There's still another group among the elderly. They have never known the Father. They've never known the Son whom the Father sent to earth to demonstrate His love. They do not understand that Jesus died so their sins can be forgiven. Like John Sornberger many people carry tremendous burdens of guilt. "God would never forgive me," they say. But He will if, in repentance and faith, they ask Him to.

The most bitter regrets can result from unkindness or failures, real or imaginary, in one's association with a loved one who has died. One may feel the chance of repentance is past.

For many regret over past failures becomes a flaming

misery. It sears the present and scars the future. To live with this type of torment saps needed energy; it also endangers health. Such people need to be able to forgive themselves.

For you to forgive yourself requires a willful decision to abdicate self-condemnation. Suppose the prodigal had said, "My father will never forgive me because I cannot forgive myself."

As difficult a decision may require that we ask persons still living to forgive us for some wrongdoing as well as to forgive those whom we feel have wronged us. It's a travesty when an older person carries a grudge he has harbored for years.

Corrie ten Boom tells how she found grace to forgive a nurse and a guard who were responsible for so much suffering she and her sister experienced. Later, learning the man who had turned traitor and betrayed the family for harboring Jews was about to be put to death because of his collaboration with the enemy, Corrie wrote telling him she forgave him and that Jesus Christ would forgive him if he asked Him to.

The man answered Corrie, telling her that her forgiveness had paved the way for him to commit his life to Christ and to ask Him for forgiveness.

Recall the Scripture: "And be kind to one another, tenderhearted, forgiving one another, even as God for Christ's sake has forgiven you." God knows all about our sins, our remorse, and our grudges. Of one woman Jesus said, "Her sins, which are many, are forgiven."

Before E. Stanley Jones died at 88, six months after suffering a stroke that left his left side paralyzed and his speech and sight impaired, he wrote: "If your life has gone to pieces, take the pieces and give them back to God, and He will make something out of them. It is amazing what God can do with a broken heart, or life, when you give Him all the pieces."[1]

If you doubt this is true, dip into the writings of C. S. Lewis, an atheist who inched his way through philosophical idealism, through pantheism, through theism, to a firm faith in Christ, the Son of the living God.

Read *The Case for Christianity,* in which Lewis insists the response to Christianity must be Yes or No. Either God exists or He does not; Christ is God or He is not; we live forever or we do not. He condones no neutrality.

No matter which category of older persons you find yourself in, God loves you. "But, the way is difficult," you say. "It's hedged by pain and suffering."

I know. Several years ago a friend, Gertrude Hanson, now deceased, helped me come to grips with suffering when she wrote a poem for me because she believed in God.

* * *

Dear tired one, pain-worn and heavy-hearted,
Look up! Look up! The Master who has charted
This way of travail, this harsh hour of testing,
Well knows your need. In striving and in questing
You will learn, through long hours of meditation,
The plan He has designed: rededication.
The still, small voice can reach you here, no stridence,
No discord will intrude. The load you carry
Will change your life. No longer ordinary,
Your life-span, be it long or short, will flower
In wonderous peace, in new-found grace and power.
Let your expectancy be joyous, changeless;
The Master will transform these hours of strangeness.[2]

* * *

Joseph Bayly tells of speaking to a group of residents in a convalescent home in Pennsylvania.[3] Recalling that one woman had said she was afraid to die, he asked: "If I could promise to take you from this home to a beautiful spring-like place where you would be forever free from all your aches and pains, where you could walk and even run, hear and see, and never have any more loneliness or sorrow ever again; but if I had to take you first through a dark tunnel to get there: how many of you would want to go?"

Almost all of the residents raised their hands.

115

Death is that tunnel. Christians need not fear it even when it seems premature.

Recently I heard Dr. Signe Berg, a medical missionary who has worked among the lepers in Taiwan, speak without rancor of her husband's assassination by the Communists in China several years ago. She said her faith in God never wavered, adding:

> Were the whole realm of nature mine,
> That were an offering far too small;
> Love so amazing, so divine,
> Demands my soul, my life, my all.[4]

During his long illness a much younger missionary planned his own funeral, insisting it be a time when God is glorified. At the memorial service the congregation honored his request and affirmed the family's faith in God when they sang, "Joyful, joyful, we adore Thee . . . ."

This is faith, faith in a dependable God who does everything right in His own time. It's the faith about which the psalmist wrote: "Yea, though I walk through the valley of the shadow of death, I will fear no evil; for Thou art with me, Thy rod and Thy staff, they comfort me. . . . Surely goodness and mercy shall follow me all the days of my life, and I will dwell in the house of the Lord forever" (Psalm 23:4, 6).

* * *

No Past Is Dead

> Sunsets in lonely windowpanes—
> God grant that when I onward go
> And night falls on this frail abode
> My spirit may reflect the glow
> From heaven's sunrise, and to know
> No past is dead, lost things He keeps.
> God will awaken that which sleeps.
>   Helga Skogsberg[5]

Appendix
Where to Go for Help

"Donor"-Card Addresses

The Eye-Bank for Sight Restoration
210 E. 64th St.
New York, N. Y. 10021

The Eye-Bank Association of America
3195 Maplewood Ave.
Winston-Salem, N. C. 27103

The American Medical Association
535 N. Dearborn St.
Chicago, Ill. 60610

Medic Alert
Turlock, Calif. 95380

The Living Bank
6631 South Main
Box 6725
Houston, Tex. 77005

Employment Opportunities

Job Retraining Program
U. S. Dept. of Labor
Washington, D. C. 20025

Action (Foster Grandparents, Peace Corps, Vista)
Washington, D. C. 20525

Gray Panthers
3700 Chestnut St.
Philadelphia, Pa. 19100

Green Thumb, Inc.
1012 14th St., N. W.
Washington, D. C. 20005

Community Action Program
Office of Economic Opportunity
Washington, D. C. 20506

National Council for Senior Citizens
1828 L. St., N. W.
Washington, D. C. 20006

National Center for Volunteer Action
1025 Massachusetts Ave., N. W.
Washington, D. C. 20336

Financial and Legal Assistance

Easy Ways to Build Family Finances and Reduce Risks and Taxes (by Fred Nauheim; Acropolis Books Ltd., Washington, D. C.)

A Woman's Money: How to Protect and Increase It in the Stock Market (by Catherine Brandt; Parker Publishing Co., Inc., West Nyack, N. Y.; out of print, available in libraries)

Sylvia Porter's Money Book (revised edition, Doubleday and Co., Inc., New York, N. Y., 1976)

National Senior Citizens Law Center
1709 W. Eighth St.
Los Angeles, Calif.

Senior Advocates, Inc.
1825 K. St., N. W.
Washington, D. C. 20006

You, the Law and Retirement (pamphlet)
Administration on Aging
U. S. Department of Health, Education and Welfare
Washington, D. C.

Health, Nutrition, etc. (information on nursing homes, foods, older folks, budgeting, etc.)

Superintendent of Documents
U. S. Government Printing Office
Washington, D. C. 20402

Group Health Association of America
1717 Massachusetts Ave., N. W.
Washington, D. C. 20036

Public Affairs Publications (pamphlets on many subjects concerning aging, health and nutrition, fads)
381 Park Ave., S.
New York, N. Y. 10006

118

Administration on AgingDept. of Health, Education and Welfare
Dept. of Health, Education and Welfare
Washington, D. C.

AARP Pharmacy Service
1274 24th St., N. W.
Washington, D. C. 20037

Hobbies/Education

People to People Hobbies, Inc.
153 Waverly Place
New York, N. Y. 10014

Letters Abroad, Inc.
45 E. 65th St.
New York, N. Y. 10021

American Craftsman's Council
29 W. 53rd St.
New York, N. Y. 10019

Institute of Lifetime Learning
1909 K. St., N. W.
Washington, D. C. 20006

215 Long Beach Blvd.
Long Beach, Calif. 90802

AARP Travel Service
555 Madison Ave.
New York, N. Y. 10022

215 Long Beach Blvd.
Long Beach, Calif. 90802

Box 14437
St. Petersburg, Fla. 33733

Information on Aging and Problems of Aging

Administration on Aging
Department of Health, Education and Welfare
Washington, D. C.

U. S. Joint Legislation Committee on Problems of Aging
Newburgh, N. Y.

Modern Maturity (magazine)
215 Long Beach Blvd.
Long Beach, Calif. 90802

Public Affairs, Inc.
22 E. 38th St.
New York, N. Y. 10016

Public Affairs Pamphlets
381 Park Ave., S.
New York, N. Y. 10016

Supt. of Documents
Library of Congress
Washington, D. C. 20025

Retirement Professional Action Group (land sales, housing,
hearing aids, health)
2000 P. St., N. W.
Washington, D. C. 20036

Listing of State Offices on Aging

Senior Advocates, Inc.
1825 K. St., N. W.
Washington, D. C. 20006

Growing Old in the Country of the Young (by Charles Percy, pp.
187—192)
McGraw-Hill Book Co.
1221 Avenue of the Americas
New York, N. Y. 10020
(also available in libraries)

Political Involvement

AARP/NRTA
1909 K. St., N. W.
Washington, D. C. 20006

National Council on Aging
1828 L. St., N. W.
Washington, D. C. 20006

Retirement Living Information

American Association of Homes for the Aged
49 W. 45th St.
New York, N. Y.

Federal Housing and Home Finance Agency
Washington, D. C.

National Council on Aging
104 E. 25th St.
New York, N. Y.

Guide to Retirement Living (book)
Rand McNally Publishing House
P. O. Box 7600
Chicago, Ill. 60680

Notes

CHAPTER 1

1. Paul Ginsbach, "Why Women Live Longer than Men," *Catholic Digest,* June 1974, pp. 36—40.
2. Alexander Leaf, M. D., *Youth in Old Age* (New York: McGraw-Hill Book Co., 1975).
3. Norman M. Lobsenz, "Sex After Sixty-five" (New York, Public Affairs Pamphlet No. 519); Ruth Winter, *Ageless Aging* (New York: Crown Publishers, 1973), ch. 9.

CHAPTER 2

1. Elmer Otte, *Rehearse Before You Retire* (Appleton, Wis. Retirement Research, 1970).
2. Paul Holter, *Guide to Retirement Living* (Chicago: Rand McNally and Co.), pp. 23—24.
3. Howard Whitman, *"Deferred Payment," The Brighter Side* (New York: Prentice Hall, Inc. 1961).

CHAPTER 3

1. Elmer Otte, *Retirement Rehearsal Guidebook* (Indianapolis: Pictorial, Inc., 1971).
2. Catharine Brandt, *A Woman's Money: How to Protect and Increase It in the Stock Market* (West Nyack, N. Y.: Parker Publishing Co., Inc., 1970). Out of print but available in libraries.
3. Catherine Marshall, *Peter Didn't Leave a Will* (New York: The Minister's and Missionary's Benefit Board, American Baptist Convention, 1957).
4. Steven Fraser, "A Check Every Month for the Rest of Your Life," *Money,* September 1973, p. 80.
5. Donald C. Bacon, "Land Frauds: Their Part in the Collapse of a Boom," *U. S. News and World Report,* Feb. 23, 1976.

CHAPTER 4

1. Paul Tournier, *Learn to Grow Old* (New York: Harper and Row Publishers, 1973), pp. 18—35.
2. Harold Dye, *No Rocking Chair for Me* (Nashville: Broadman Press, 1975).
3. Ralph Seager (used by permission of author).

4. Bulletin No. 1223, *Comparative Job Performance by Age* (Washington, D. C.: Dept. of Labor).

CHAPTER 5

1. John Baillie, *A Diary of Private Prayer* (Charles Scribner's Sons, 597 Fifth Ave., New York, N. Y.), 1949.
2. Henry Jacobson, "Get Yourself Involved," *Power for Living* (Scripture Press, 1825 College Ave., Wheaton, Ill.), 1976.

CHAPTER 6

1. Alexander Leaf, M. D., *Youth in Old Age* (New York: McGraw-Hill Book Co., 1975), pp. xiv—xv.
2. Edward J. Sieglitz, M. D., "The Personal Challenge of Aging: Biological Changes and Maintenance of Health," *Aging in Today's Society,* pp. 44—53.
3. Charles C. Edwards, M. D., "What You Can Do to Combat High Blood Pressure," *Today's Health,* November 1975, pp. 24—26.
4. Siegmund H. May, M. D., *The Growing Years* (Philadelphia/N. Y.: J. B. Lippincott Co., 1968), p. 87.
5. Lawrence Galton, "Is a Vital Ingredient Missing from Your Diet?" *Reader's Digest,* December 1974, pp. 105—09.

CHAPTER 7

1. "The Role of Stress and What to Do About It," *High Blood Pressure . . .* © 1975 by Frank A. Finnerty Jr., M. D., and Shirley M. Linde (David McKay Co., Inc.).
2. *The Journal of Psychosomatic Research,* II, 214—15.

CHAPTER 9

1. *Science News,* Sept. 18, 1972.
2. James C. Folsom, M. D., and Geneva S. Folsom, Ed. D., "The Real World" (Tuscaloosa, Ala.: Manual Arts Therapy Print Clinic, summer 1975).
3. James C. Folsom, M. D., "Intensive Hospital Therapy for Geriatric Patients," *Current Psychiatric Therapies, Volume 7,* ed. Jules H. Massermann, M. D. (New York: Grune & Stratton, 1967), pp. 209—15.

CHAPTER 10

1. Bernard E. Nash, Executive Director of NRTA/AARP, "Home Health Care: A Much Better Way."
2. Janet Love, "The Alternative to Hospitals," *Modern Maturity,* April/May 1976, pp. 29—30.
3. Charles H. Percy, *Growing Old in the Country of the Young* (New York: McGraw-Hill Book Co., 1974).

CHAPTER 11

1. Hugh Beaumont, "A Thing to Remember," *Ladies' Home Journal,* January 1958.

2. Arnold Toynbee, *Man's Concern with Death* (New York: McGraw-Hill Book Co., 1968).
3. Elisabeth Kubler-Ross, M. D., *On Death and Dying* (New York: Macmillan Publishing Co., 1969).
4. "Life or Death," *U. S. News and World Report,* May 22, 1972.
5. C. S. Lewis, *A Grief Observed* (Seabury Press, 1963).
6. Joseph Bayly, *Psalms of My Life* (Wheaton, Ill.: Tyndale Publishing Co., 1969), pp. 24—25.

CHAPTER 12

1. E. Stanley Jones, revised and arranged by his daughter Eunice Jones Matthews, *The Divine Yes* (Nashville: Abingdon Press, 1975).
2. © Margaret J. Anderson.
3. Joseph Bayly, *The View from a Hearse* (Elgin, Ill.: David C. Cook Publishing Co., 1969), pp. 84—85.
4. Isaac Watts, "When I Survey the Wondrous Cross," last stanza.
5. Helga Skogsberg, *Songs of Pilgrimage* (Chicago: Covenant Press, 1962), p. 113. Used by permission.

Bibliography

Armond, Glen. "Safety, Liquidity, Yield—Money Market Funds Are Here to Stay," *Barron's,* Oct. 6, 1975.

Atchley, Robert. *The Social Forces in Later Life.* Belmont, Calif.: Wadsworth Publishing Co., Inc., 1972.

Baillie John. *A Diary of Private Prayer.* New York: Charles Scribner's Sons, 1949.

Bayly, Joseph. *Psalms of My Life.* Wheaton, Ill.: Tyndale Publishing Co., 1969.

———*The View from a Hearse.* Elgin, Ill.: David C. Cook Publishing House, 1969.

Bengtson, Vern L. *The Social Psychology of the Aging.* Indianapolis/New York: Bobbs-Merrill Co., Inc. 1973.

Brandt, Catharine. *A Woman's Money: How to Protect and Increase It in the Stock Market* (West Nyack, N. Y.: Parker Publishing Co., Inc., 1970). Out of print.

Committees on Aging. *Mental Health and the Elderly.* Washington, D. C.: U. S. Government Printing Office, 1975.

Curtin, Sharon R., *Nobody Ever Died of Old Age (In Praise of Old People; in Outrage at Their Loneliness).* Boston/Toronto: Little, Brown and Company, 1972.

Davis, Richards H. *Aging: Prospects and Issues.* Los Angeles: The University of Southern California Press, 1973.

Dye, Harold C. *No Rocking Chair for Me.* Nashville: Broadman Press, 1975.

Fraser, Steven. "A Check Every Month for the Rest of Your Life," *Money,* September 1975, pp. 77—80.

Holter, Paul. *Guide to Retirement Living.* Chicago: Rand McNally and Co., 1972.

Irwin, Theodore. *Living with a Heart Ailment.* New York: Public Affairs Pamphlets, 1975.

Jones, E. Stanley, revised and arranged by his daughter Eunice Jones Mathews. *The Divine Yes.* Nashville: Abingdon Press, 1975.

Kubler-Ross, Elisabeth. *On Death and Dying.* New York: Macmillan Publishing Co., 1969.

Leaf, Alexander, M. D. *Youth in Old Age.* New York: MrGraw-Hill Book Co., 1975.

Levinsohn, Florence, M. S., in consultation with Daniel Streicher, M. D. *A Doctor Talks to Older Patients.* Chicago: Budlong Press Company, 1965.

Lewis, C. S. *A Grief Observed.* Seabury Press, 1963.

Nauheim, Fred. *Easy Ways to Build Family Finances and Reduce Risks and Taxes.* Washington, D. C.: Acropolis Books, Ltd. 1973.

May, Sigmund H. *The Growing Years.* Philadelphia/N. Y: J. B. Lippincott, Co., 1968.

Moss, Gordon and Walter Moss, eds. *Growing Old.* New York: Simon & Schuster Pocket Books, 1975.

Otte, Elmer. *Rehearse Before You Retire.* Appleton, Wis.: Retirement Research, 1970.

_____*Retirement Rehearsal Guidebook.* Indianapolis: Pictorial, Inc., 1971, 1974.

Percy, Charles H. *Growing Old in the Country of the Young.* New York: McGraw-Hill Book Co., 1974.

Porter, Sylvia. *Sylvia Porter's Money Book.* New York: Doubleday and Co., Inc., 1976.

Public Affairs Pamphlets Nos. 172, 377A, 446, 286, 485, 519.

Sieglitz, Edward J., M. D. "The Personal Challenge of Aging: Biological Changes and Maintenance of Health," *Aging in Today's Society,* pp. 44—53.

Skogsberg, Helga. *Songs of Pilgrimage.* Chicago: Covenant Press, 1962.

Smith, Bert Kruger. *Aging in America.* Dubuque: Wm. C. Brown Publishers, 1975.

Stern, Edith M. *A Full Life After 65.* New York: Public Affairs Pamphlet No. 347, 1976.

Tournier, Paul. *Learn to Grow Old.* New York/London: Harper and Row Publishers, 1973.

Toynbee, Arnold. *Man's Concern with Death.* New York: McGraw-Hill Book Co., 1968.

Whitman, Howard. *"Deferred Payment," The Brighter Side.* New York: Prentice Hall, Inc., 1961.

Winter, Ruth. *Ageless Aging.* New York: Crown Publishers, Inc., 1973.